Crafty Ideas for the Bride on a Budget

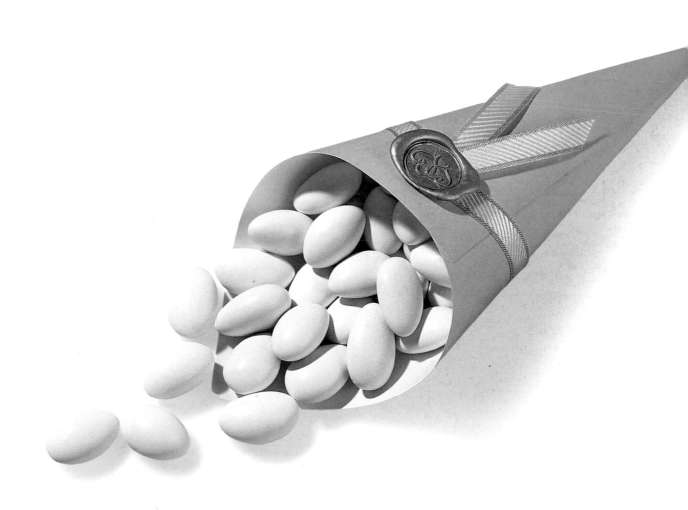

Crafty Ideas for the Bride on a Budget

75 DIY Wedding Projects

Edited by
Linda Kopp

LARK BOOKS

A Division of Sterling Publishing Co., Inc.
New York / London

Editor: Linda Kopp
Art Director: Megan Kirby
Cover Designer: Barbara Zaretsky
Contributing Writers: Kathy Sheldon, Karen Free,
          Karen Backstein, Ruth Planey, Susan Kieffer, Rebecca Guthrie
Photo Styling: Megan Kirby, Skip Wade
Art Production Assistant: Shannon Yokeley, Jeff Hamilton, Bradley Norris
Editorial Assistance: Rebecca Guthrie
Editorial Intern: Kelly J. Johnson
Illustrator: Orin Lundgren
Photographer: Keith Wright

The Library of Congress has cataloged the hardcover edition as follows:

Michaels book of wedding crafts / edited by Linda Kopp.
     p. cm.
   Includes index.
   ISBN 1-57990-639-7 (hardcover)
   1. Handicraft. 2. Wedding decorations. I. Kopp, Linda. II. Michaels (Firm). III. Title.
TT149.M53 2006
745.594'1--dc22

                                                   2006015067

10 9 8 7 6 5 4 3 2 1

Published by Lark Books, A Division of Sterling Publishing Co., Inc.
387 Park Avenue South, New York, N.Y. 10016

First Paperback Edition 2010
Text © 2006, Lark Books, A Division of Sterling Publishing Co., Inc.
Photography © 2006, Lark Books, A Division of Sterling Publishing Co., Inc.
Illustrations © 2006, Lark Books, A Division of Sterling Publishing Co., Inc.
Lace background image on cover © 2010 Jupiterimages Corporation

Previously published as Michaels Book of Wedding Crafts

Distributed in Canada by Sterling Publishing,
c/o Canadian Manda Group, 165 Dufferin Street
Toronto, Ontario, Canada M6K 3H6

Distributed in the United Kingdom by GMC Distribution Services,
Castle Place, 166 High Street, Lewes, East Sussex, England BN7 1XU

Distributed in Australia by Capricorn Link (Australia) Pty Ltd., P.O. Box 704, Windsor, NSW 2756 Australia

If you have questions or comments about this book, please contact:
Lark Books, 67 Broadway, Asheville, NC 28801
(828) 253-0467

Manufactured in China

ISBN 13: 978-1-57990-807-2 (hardcover) 978-1-60059-689-6 (paperback)

For information about custom editions, special sales, premium and corporate purchases, please contact
Sterling Special Sales Department at 800-805-5489 or specialsales@sterlingpub.com.

For information about desk and examination copies available to college and
university professors, requests must be submitted to academic@larkbooks.com.
Our complete policy can be found at www.larkbooks.com.

To all the brides who are crafting their own wedding memories.

Table of Contents

Menu

Appendix

Introduction

Here Comes the (Budget-Conscious) Bride

A meaningful, beautiful wedding doesn't have to capsize your wallet. Each of us wants our wedding to be the perfect blend of authentic style and mindful affordability, and it's often challenging to pair these elements in a world of over-the-top extravaganza weddings. Enter *Crafty Ideas for the Bride on a Budget,* your guide to expressing yourself *and* being clever with your finances.

With 75 projects and countless springboards for inspiration, this union of DIY and "I do" offers you an abundance of solutions. Delight family and friends with true-to-you save the date cards; share handmade gifts with your bridesmaids; guide guests to reception tables with stylized centerpieces; and savor your wedding memories in a personalized photo album. Short on time? Never fear. Quick & Easy projects are featured throughout to help you whip up bridal innovation in a flash.

Whether your style is classically opulent, simply chic, or dynamically bold, you'll get to the heart of your big day with creative takes on tradition and originality. *Crafty Ideas for the Bride on a Budget* offers five themed styles to inspire your handcrafted wedding. The Glamour chapter features an abundance of rich fabrics and sumptuous details, Pretty in Pink adds sweet romance to the day, and Modern Pastels celebrates the inspiration of flowers. Your effervescent spirit is echoed in the merriment of Fanciful & Fun, and Bold & Bright speaks to the vibrant side of celebration.

Let your imagination and know-how nature fall in love with these creative, celebratory projects. Before you know it, you and your budget will tie the knot.

12-Month Wedding Planner

12 Months

- Announce your engagement to family and friends
- Send your announcement to local newspapers
- Purchase a planning notebook or software
- Plan a preliminary budget

11 Months

- Research wedding and reception locations
- Select bridal party and ask each person to participate
- Settle on a wedding site

10 Months

- Set your date
- Send out save-the-date cards
- Book the reception location
- Interview and select the caterer, photographer, florist, musicians, videographer, and wedding director
- Develop a guest list
- Start reviewing invitations

9 Months

- Register for gifts
- Begin wedding dress shopping

8 Months

- Select the priest, minister, pastor, rabbi, or judge
- Sample cakes and select your cake design
- Begin to review honeymoon locations
- Finalize overall budget

- Choose wedding veil
- Start thinking about flowers

7 Months

- Order wedding dress
- Begin to shop for bridesmaid dresses
- Finalize guest list

6 Months

- Begin shopping for invitations and stationery
- Place order for bridesmaid dresses and accessories
- Bride and groom's mother select dresses
- Reserve rental equipment (chairs, arches, linens, etc.)
- Order or make invitations and stationery

5 Months

- Review favor design
- Shop for wedding rings
- Finalize your décor ideas and shop for or make decorations
- Begin shopping for groom's wedding attire
- Send tux measurement forms to groomsmen
- Finalize dates for bachelorette parties and showers
- Reserve rehearsal dinner site

4 Months

- Finalize flowers
- Order tuxes
- Book honeymoon

- Purchase groom's gift
- Schedule appointments for trial hair and makeup
- Book block of rooms for out-of-town guests

3 Months

- Select favors
- Finalize vows
- Plan seating arrangements for reception
- Purchase or make wedding accessories, such as guest book, ring bearer pillow, toasting glasses, unity candle, flower basket, serving set
- Choose or write vows
- Book hair, nail, and makeup appointments
- Ceremony program

2 Months

- Mail invitations
- Purchase or make gifts for bridal party
- Schedule first fitting
- Apply for marriage license
- Attend showers

1 Month

- Finalize ceremony plans
- Submit wedding program to stationer
- Finalize transportation of family, party and out-of-town guests
- Pick up wedding rings
- Make arrangements for bridesmaid luncheon

- Get forms for name change on driver's license, Social Security card, insurance and medical plans, and bank accounts
- Schedule second bridal fitting

3 Weeks

- Reconfirm hotel reservations for guests as well as for honeymoon
- Purchase or make dinner seating cards for guests

2 Weeks

- Pack for honeymoon
- Send final payment to suppliers
- Get hair trimmed

1 Week

- Pick up gown and accessories
- Gather wedding accessories; put in bag or box ready to go
- Attend bachelor or bachelorette parties
- Attend rehearsal and rehearsal dinner
- Make time to relax

The Bride's Guide to Basic Crafting Tools & Materials

Crafting is the perfect way to personalize a wedding. Many of the projects in this book are simple, and thus ideal for the first-time and novice crafter. If you're new to crafting, it might be helpful to take a moment and review the tools and materials below. An illustrated guide to basic craft techniques and working with fondant can be found on pages 172–193.

Bone folders

Bone folders easily make crisp, professional creases in hand-made cards and invitations.

Card stock

This sturdy, heavy-weight paper is perfect when making thank-you cards, invitations, and place cards.

Decorative-edge scissors

Quickly dress up the edge of any paper with decorative edge scissors. A wide variety of pretty edge designs are available.

Embossing inks & powder

Embossing creates a raised design on paper or metal. Embossing inks are especially designed to dry slowly on paper enabling embossing powders to melt and fuse with stamped images when heat is applied.

Embossing powder is made from tiny plastic pellets. When sprinkled over a stamped image and hot air from a heat gun is applied, the pellets melt, forming a raised surface.

Eyelets

Eyelets are small, colorful rings of metal used to attach photographs, embellishments, or decorative paper to another surface. The eyelet's center hole allows ribbon or other decorative materials to be threaded through.

Fondant

Fondant is a sugary syrup that has been crystallized to a smooth, satiny pie-crust consistency. It can be manipulated like

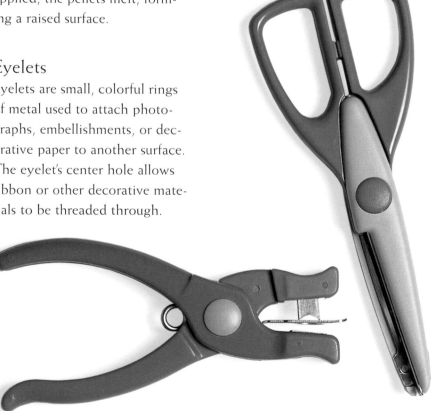

play dough and is used to cover cakes, and to make elaborate cake decorations.

Paper mache

Paper mache is made into forms of all shapes and sizes. It is made out of a mixture of paper pulp and paste, and when purchased at a store, is normally brown in color.

Paint pen

Paint pens are quick-drying and non-bleeding, and come in many colors including gold and silver metallic. They are used to create decorative accents on glass, wood, porcelain, plastic, metal and paper.

Paper punches

Paper punches are handy tools that are similar to a standard hole-punch, but can produce an array of shapes. Choose from a multitude of designs ranging from ovals and squares, to flowers and specialty shapes.

Scrapbooking paper

Most scrapbooking paper is of medium-weight and can be used in many projects. Scrapbooking paper is available in a seemingly endless array of patterns, colors, and textures.

Seal

A seal is a metal stamp with a raised or engraved symbol that is pressed into melted wax leaving the symbol's impression.

Stamps

A stamp has a raised design that is used in combination with an inkpad to make decorative patterns on paper.

Sticker machine

A sticker/lamination machine easily turns most any flat-surfaced material (less than 1/16 inch thick), such as paper, magnets, or fabric into a sticker. The machine applies an adhesive to the back, eliminating the need for glue.

Vellum

Vellum is a transparent, light-weight paper used for layering and for creating special effects. It is also available in colors and subtle patterns.

Glamour

What is glamour? It's glorious excess, with yards of rich fabrics, captivating to the eye and irresistible to the touch. It's a bounty of pearls and shiny jewels, and a garden of flawless, fragrant roses and other lush blossoms creating a vision of beauty everywhere. That's glamour—and it makes any bride feel extra special, like a Hollywood star or a model on the cover of a magazine.

Such opulence looks expensive, but creating a sumptuous wedding needn't cost a king's ransom—just a little creativity and style. So think glittering, lavish opulence—think glamorous, and your wedding day dreams will come true.

Vellum Overlay Invitation

A graceful monogram becomes a subtle design element
when tucked under a gossamer sheet of vellum. Adding
a thin silver border to the invitation is a quick way
to add a touch of sparkle to a kit-purchased invitation.

How To Make It

Materials

Blank embossed invitation

Sheet of clear vellum

Pearl-edged ribbon, about ¼ yard

Sealing wax and seal
 (optional, see step 6)

Tools & Supplies

Computer and printer

Silver marker or pen

Straightedge

Scissors or paper trimmer

Hole punch

Matches (optional, see step 6)

Tip *Craft supply stores sell embossed
invitation kits that include
invitations, envelopes, response
cards, and sometimes even items
such as ribbon and vellum.
These kits make it easy by
including instructions for
using your computer, invitation
wording examples, and test sheets.*

1 Choose your font and then use the computer and printer to print a large monogrammed initial into the center of the embossed invitation.

2 Draw a line around the inside of the embossed edges using the silver marker or pen and the straightedge.

3 Using the computer, choose your font, and then type your invitation text, centering the margins. Print the text onto the sheet of vellum. Measure the inside silver rectangle you drew onto the invitation. Cut the vellum into a rectangle just slightly smaller than this measurement.

4 To create the holes to attach the ribbon, carefully position the vellum over the invitation, and then punch two holes through both sheets, centered at the top and about 1 inch apart.

5 Make the bow by first threading each end of the pearl-edged ribbon through the holes from the front side of the card to the back. Cross the ribbon ends on the back side of the card, and then pull each through the opposite side's hole. Tighten the bow, and trim each end with a diagonal cut.

6 To make a wax seal, follow the manufacturer's instructions and drip wax on an envelope flap. Gently press the seal stamp on the wax, then remove it with a slight rocking motion.

Designer: Brandy Logan

Mr. and Mrs. William R. Luckey
invite you to share in the ceremony
uniting their daughter

Laura Michelle
to
Steve Allen Robbins

on Saturday, the twenty-first of October
two thousand and six
at two o'clock in the afternoon
First Presbyterian Church
512 Grove St.
Memphis, Tennessee

Stately Silver Urn

Prepare for a symphony of oohs and ahs when guests first glimpse this magnificent centerpiece. The jewel-draped urn is a grand vessel housing 50 white roses.

Materials

12-inch-diameter plastic urn, 18 inches tall

Plastic spray primer

Silver spray paint

Black acrylic paint

Clear gloss spray

15 lb. bead-stringing wire

7 plastic crystals, 1¼ inches in length

7 pieces of floral wire, 10 inches long

Package of string pearls

7 beads, ¼-inch diameter

50 silk roses

6-inch-wide tulle (optional)

Tools & Supplies

Paintbrush

Clean rag

Paper towels

Measuring tape

Drill and small drill bit

Wire cutters

Scissors

Hot glue and glue gun

Designer: Joan K. Morris

How To Make It

1 Following the manufacturer's instructions, spray the urn with plastic primer. Let dry.

2 Apply a coat of silver spray paint over the primer. Let dry.

3 To "antique" the urn, mix equal parts water and black acrylic paint. Working in a small area, paint the urn with the mixture and then rub it off with a soft rag. Continue the process over the entire urn, leaving the lines and crevices of the urn dark. Let dry.

4 Spray with clear gloss spray to seal. Let dry.

5 To figure out spacing for the crystals, measure around the top edge of the urn and divide the measurement by seven. That number is how many inches apart your crystals should be placed. Our spacing was every 5¾ inches. Using your measurement, mark and drill holes about ¾ inch down from the top or just under the lip of the rim.

6 Cut seven 12-inch pieces of beading wire. At one end of each wire attach a crystal, tying two square knots. Place a dab of hot glue at the end of each knot. Run the other end through the hole at the top of the urn, and wrap the wire around and back through the hole, tying two more square knots. Place a dab of hot glue at the end of the knot. The crystal should be hanging down about four inches.

7 To make the dual rows of draped pearls, cut seven pieces of floral wire, each 10 inches in length. Start at one end of the string pearls and measure 10 inches. Place a piece of wire at that point and twist it around the pearls a couple of times to keep it in place. Repeat this process for each hole you drilled. Next measure seven inches of pearls, and connect that string to the first with the wire. Work your way around to the end again.

8 To place the draped pearls on the urn, run the wire through the holes to the inside of the urn. Thread one end of the wire through a ¼-inch bead, and twist it together with the other end. Repeat the step with each hole all the way around the urn.

9 Hot-glue a string of pearls around the lip of the rim, covering the holes, and another string around the base of the urn.

10 Place all the roses into the urn at once and arrange them to your liking, bending the leaves to make them look natural.

11 If desired, loosely tuck pieces of tulle around the rim of the arrangement and loops of tulle between some of the roses.

Satin Ring Pillow

This ring pillow is truly befitting of a fairy tale wedding.
Nested simply in the middle of snowy white satin, the
wedding bands are illuminated by lustrous crystals.

Materials

Satin fabric, ½ yard

Thread, in a matching color

Pillow form, 12 x 12 inches

Braided bead thread

5 Swarovski crystal sliders

5 small two-hole buttons

Yard of satin ribbon, ⅛ inch wide

Tools & Supplies

Ruler

Scissors

Straight pins

Sewing machine

Sewing needle

Large-eyed embroidery needle

Designer: Joan K. Morris

No-Sew Pillow

If you're short on time (or sewing skills!), simply purchase a ring pillow and decorate it yourself, referring to steps 5–8 as a guide.

How To Make It

1 Cut the satin into two 12 x 12-inch squares. Place the squares right sides together, and pin them, leaving a 5-inch opening on one side.

2 Machine stitch with a ½-inch seam allowance around all edges, but leave the 5-inch opening. Backstitch at each end of the opening to reinforce it, since this is where you'll push the pillow through. Clip the corners.

3 Turn the pillowcase right side out, and stuff the pillow form into the satin cover, making sure the corners of the form are pushed into the corners of the cover. It should be a tight fit.

4 Stitch the 5-inch opening closed by hand, hiding the stitches.

5 To tuft the pillow, thread the embroidery needle with the bead thread, push the needle through the center of the pillow, out the other side, and then back up about ⅛ of an inch over. Pull the thread very tight and tie it in a couple of square knots (right over left and left over right). Repeat this four more times to make the tufts toward each corner of the pillow (see photo for placement).

6 Next you'll attach a crystal slider to the front and a button to the back of each tuft. To begin, thread the sewing needle with thread doubled and knotted at the ends. Starting at the center tuft at the back of the pillow, push the needle up through the pillow to the front. Run the threaded needle through one of the four holes in the side of one crystal slider. Push the needle and thread back down to the pillow's bottom, through one hole in a button, up through the other button hole, and then through the pillow and into another hole in the crystal slider. Repeat this until you've stitched through all four holes in the crystal slider. End with the thread at the button. Knot several times, hiding the knots under the button.

7 Repeat this to attach crystal sliders and buttons to the rest of the tufts.

8 Thread the ⅛-inch ribbon under the center crystal, and tie it in a bow.

Cascading Pearl Favor Box

Perched on pearl feet and with mounds of pearls spilling over its top, this favor box would make an oyster envious. Hot-glue a decorative paper clip to the back of the lid, and this box serves double duty as a place card holder.

How To Make It

1 Paint the inside and outside of the box with the silver spray paint. Let dry.

2 Measure and cut a piece of foil to fit around the edge of the box's lid. Measure and cut a piece of foil to fit around the outside of the box itself. Turn the box over and lightly draw around the lid onto the foil. Cut about ½ inch out from the pencil line to create a piece of foil that's slightly larger than the top.

3 Trace the template on page 194.

4 Use masking tape to tape the piece of foil that fits over the lid's edge to the piece that fits over the outside of the box. Place this, shiny-side-down, on a slightly soft surface (most mousepads work well). Set the traced template onto the foil and trace the design with the embossing tool, pressing hard enough to mark the foil but not too hard—you can tear it. Remove the tracing paper and emboss the design again, pressing harder this time.

5 Paint a layer of craft glue on the top of the box. Place the round piece on the top of the box's lid, and fold the edges over using the other end of the tool to flatten out the foil.

Materials

Round wooden box,
 3½ inches in diameter

Silver spray paint

Lightweight aluminum tooling foil

Assorted pearls (seed to ¾ inch)

Shaped clips (aluminum swirl)

Place card

Tools & Supplies

Measuring tape

Scissors

Pencil

Template (page 194)

Photocopier or tracing paper
 and pencil

Masking tape

Embossing tool
 (usually comes with foil)

1-inch paintbrush

Craft glue

Quick-set epoxy

Needle-nose pliers

Hot glue and glue gun

Designer: Joan K. Morris

6 Paint a layer of craft glue on the outside of the box. Untape the two strips of embossed foil, and lay the large piece in place on the outside of the box, making sure the side you drew on goes against the box (you want the other side to show). Rub lightly to push into place, making sure the top edge isn't higher than the top edge of the box.

7 Paint a layer of craft glue on the edge of the lid. Line up the design of the foil strip with the bottom edge and press into place, again making sure the side you drew on goes against the box. Rub lightly to push into place. Let dry.

8 Using the epoxy, glue four evenly spaced ½-inch pearls to the bottom of the box to serve as feet. Let dry.

9 Use the epoxy to attach the assorted-size pearls to the top of the lid. Start with a layer of smaller pearls in the center, and glue the larger pearls on top of them. It helps to use the needle-nose pliers to place the smaller pearls. Just grab a pearl with the pliers, dip one end into the glue, and then place it on the box.

10 Use hot glue to attach a shaped clip onto the back of the box so one end shows above the lid. Slide a place card into the clip. (If you use hot glue, guests will be able to pull the clip off and use the box after the wedding.)

Formal Unity Candle Set

When lit, the flickering flames of these candles will illuminate the richness of the pearls and crystals, enhancing the beauty of the union. After decorating these candles, store them upright in a cool place to prevent the tapers from bending.

Materials

White pillar candle, 9 inches tall

2 white taper candles, 9 inches tall

2 glass taper holders, 2 inches tall

Lightweight embossing aluminum tooling foil

Package of pearl-headed corsage pins

Aluminum wire, 28-gauge

16 Swarovski crystal sliders

Package of 4mm pearl beads

Tools & Supplies

Measuring tape

Straightedge

Scissors

Templates (page 194)

Photocopier or tracing paper and pencil

Embossing tool (usually comes with the foil)

Wire cutters

Designer: Joan K. Morris

How To Make It

1 Measure the pillar candle's circumference. Cut a 3-inch-wide strip of foil that's as long as the candle's circumference plus 1 inch.

2 Photocopy the pillar template on page 194, enlarging or reducing if needed to get the design to fit on your strip of foil. (You can instead use tracing paper and a pencil to make a copy of the template.) Place the foil strip, shiny side down, on a slightly soft surface (most mousepads work well). Position the pattern over the foil strip and use the embossing tool to trace over the design, pressing hard enough to mark the foil but not too hard—you can tear it. Remove the pattern and retrace the design, pressing harder this time.

Glamour

3 Fold the top and bottom over ½ inch and the edges in ¼ inch toward the side you drew on.

4 Use the wire cutters to cut the shafts of the pearl-headed corsage pins to ½ inch. (Save the parts you cut off—you'll use them later.) Wrap the foil strip, finished side out, around the pillar. Place it about halfway up, letting the ends overlap slightly. Push the pearl-headed cut pins through the top and bottom edges of the foil and into the candle, spaced 1 inch apart.

5 Repeat steps 1 through 4 for both tapers, but make the foil strip only 1½ inches wide, use the taper template, and fold the tops and bottoms under only ¼ inch.

6 Cut a piece of wire a couple of inches longer than the pillar candle's circumference. String on one of the slider crystals. Now add pearl beads and three more evenly spaced crystals to completely encircle the pillar. (For our candle this meant eight pearl beads between each crystal slider.) When you have the right amount for the wire to fit snugly on the candle, thread one of the wire ends through the next crystal and twist the ends together to form a ring. Snip off any excess wire, and hide the knot behind the crystal.

7 Slide the decorated wire ring onto the candle, and hold it in place about 1 inch above the foil band by pressing the ends of the corsage pins into the candle beneath the wire on either side of each crystal slider. (Use the wire cutters to push the cut shafts into the candle.) Make another crystal-and-pearl ring and attach it about 1 inch below the foil band.

8 Repeat steps 6 and 7 to make and attach two pearl-and-crystal rings for both of the tapers, this time using only 2 crystal sliders on each ring.

9 Place the tapers in the glass holders.

The Meaning of Unity Candles

The lighting of unity candles is meant as romantic imagery, a symbol suggestive of the couple's individual lives brought together as one bond. It's thought to be an American tradition, which probably began during the 1960s.

There are a variety of ways to perform the ceremony: the bride and groom simultaneously light the unity candle with their own smaller candle, which was either lit by themselves or by their parents or grandparents. You could also have each guest or member of the wedding party pass a lit candle to one another until all the flames are lit. The couple would then light their unity candle as a symbol of the two families merging. Some couples choose to blow out their individual candles, while others leave all three candles lit, depending on how they view the symbolism. The lighting of the candle is usually accompanied by music or poetry.

Since the unity candle is not a typical religious tradition, be sure to let your officiant know that you wish to incorporate it into the ceremony. The candles are generally used in Protestant ceremonies or in weddings not held in a church.

If you're quite charmed by incorporating symbols of unity, but don't wish to have a candle-lighting ceremony, there are lots of options. Look to other family customs or even other cultures for inspiration.

Silver Cup with Monogram Seal

A silver cup is a classic gift, reserved for milestone celebrations. Filled with chocolates, mints, or fresh flowers, these favors make timeless mementos.

Materials

Silver cup

12 inches of pearl-edged ribbon, 2 inches wide

Silver sealing wax

Monogram stamp

Tools & Supplies

Scissors

Hot glue and glue gun

Tin foil

Spatula

How To Make It

1 Wrap ribbon around the cup, and cut to the exact length.

2 To keep the ribbon in place, secure it to the back of the cup with a spot of hot glue at the top and bottom edge of the ribbon. Wrap the ribbon around to the front and create some pleats by pinching the ends. Hot-glue in place, making sure the pleats are flat and the ribbon measures about an inch wide.

3 Fold a piece of tin foil in half. This is the base of your wax seal. Practice to get the correct shape and size. Light the sealing wax candle and, following the manufacturer's instructions, let the wax drip into a circle on the tin foil. Press the stamp into the center of the circle, and pull away. Once you have created a shape and imprint that you like, gently push the spatula under the wax and lift it up.

4 Hot-glue the wax seal over the center of the pleats where the ribbon ends join together.

Designer: Joan K. Morris

Crystalline Rose Bouquet Cake

Like the glistening of the sun off freshly fallen snow, this cake shimmers with delicate sugar flakes. A cluster of porcelain-looking fondant roses graces two of the tiers, completing the timeless look.

Materials

Three cake layers:

12-inch round cake, 4 inches tall

10-inch round cake, 4 inches tall

8-inch round cake, 4 inches tall

Buttercream icing (see page 193)

Confectioner's sugar

48 ounces of white fondant (for 12-inch layer)

36 ounces of white fondant (for 10-inch layer)

24 ounces of white fondant (for 8-inch layer)

24 ounces of white fondant (to create the roses)

Cake board, 12-inch diameter

Cake board, 10-inch diameter

Cake board, 8-inch diameter

Wooden dowel, ¼-inch diameter

10-12 jars of white sugar cake crystals

Thinned fondant adhesive (see recipe on page 193), or royal icing (see recipe on page 96)

Designer: Joan K. Morris

Tools & Supplies

Cake leveler or serrated knife

Cake decorating turntable

Large angled spatula

Large rolling pin

Gridded roll and cut cake mat

Fondant smoothing tool

Spray bottle (with a "light mist" setting)

Cornstarch

Sharp knife

Scissors

How To Make It

1 Follow the cake instructions, and bake, cool, level, and ice the cake layers with buttercream icing (refer to pages 178–180).

2 Cover the cake layers with fondant (see pages 180–181).

3 Stack the cake layers (refer to pages 183–184).

4 Sprinkle cake crystals over the top and sides of the cake. If the crystals do not stick, lightly mist the fondant with water from a spray bottle, and then apply the crystals.

5 Once all surfaces of the cake are evenly covered with crystals, refer to the Ribbon Roses and Full Bloom Roses sections on pages 191–192 and begin making the roses. Make roses of varying sizes and group them in a bouquet-fashion using the project photo as a guide. Attach the roses to the cake using thinned fondant adhesive or Royal Icing.

Tip *Each 4-inch cake layer can be made using two 2-inch layers*

Framed
Save-the-Date
Magnet

Your wedding date is sure to remain top-of-mind
with all the recipients of this handy yet pretty magnet.
These announcements are quick and easy to make when you
purchase a kit complete with envelopes and blank embossed cards.

We are getting married, so be sure to save the date!

Laura and Steve

October 21, 2006

First Presbyterian Church
Memphis, Tennessee

Laura and Steve
October 21, 2006

Designer: Brandy Logan

Materials

Card stock, 8½ x 11 inches

Small metal frame

Cellophane tape

Adhesive-backed magnet sheet

12 inches of stranded mini pearls

3 miniature rhinestones

3 silk blossoms

Blank embossed invitation

Adhesive dots

Envelope

Sheet of floral embossed paper

Tools

Computer and printer

Scissors

Craft knife

Hot glue and glue gun

Silver marker or pen

Straightedge

Glue stick

How To Make It

1 Using the computer, choose your font, and then type a large monogram that will fit inside the metal frame's window onto the sheet of card stock. The monogram should be gray. If you don't have a color printer, you can type the monogram in any color and print it in black and white. (You may need to experiment a bit to find which color prints as the best gray.)

2 Type the couple's names and the wedding date, making sure this text is centered so it will print over the monogram and will fit inside your metal frame's window. Put the monogrammed card stock back into the printer and print the names and date right on top of the gray monogram.

3 Cut out around the text, leaving a border that's smaller than the frame but larger than the frame's window. Tape the card stock to the back of the frame, making sure the text is centered in its window.

4 Remove the protective paper from the adhesive-backed magnet sheet and set the frame on top of it so the back of the frame sticks to the back of the magnet. Use the craft knife to trim around all edges.

5 Use the hot glue gun to attach the strand of mini pearls around the frame's window. Hot-glue one of the rhinestones to the center of one of the silk flowers and then attach the flower to the upper left corner of the frame.

6 Decorate the embossed invitation by using the silver pen or marker to draw a line inside the embossed rectangle. Attach the magnet to the card with adhesive dots.

7 Use your computer and printer to type and print "We are getting married, so be sure to save the date," your names, and the wedding date on the front of the envelope.

8 Cut the floral embossed paper into two thin strips the same length as your envelope. Attach one near the top and one near the bottom of the envelope's front, using the glue stick. Use hot glue to attach a rhinestone to the centers of both remaining silk blossoms. Hot-glue one blossom to the right of the top silver strip and one blossom to the left of the bottom silver strip.

Dear Aunt Judy,

Thank you so very much for the exquisite picture frame that you gave us in honor of
our wedding. We are happy to have such a beautiful piece to frame our favorite
wedding photo in. We plan on hanging it over our mantle in the living room.

Give our love to your family for us, and we'll see you all very soon.

Love,
Laura and Steve

Pearl-Trimmed Thank You Note Card

A simple string of pearls is always fashionable, and this card is no exception. To ensure that the embellishments do not inhibit your writing, script your note of gratitude first, then add the pearls and the rhinestone-dotted monogram.

How To Make It

Materials

Embossed card,
  3-½ x 5-½ inches

Stranded mini pearls,
  about ½ yard

Metal monogram

3 miniature rhinestones

Tools & Supplies

Silver pen or marker

Straightedge

Scissors

Hot glue and glue gun

Wire cutters

Designer: Brandy Logan

1 Handwrite or use a computer and printer to print your note of thanks on the embossed 3½ x 5½-inch card, making sure to leave a blank space in the lower right corner.

2 Use the silver pen or maker and the straightedge to draw a line around the inside of the embossed edges.

3 Cut the strand of mini pearls to fit inside the silver line (use photo as reference). Attach the strand using the hot glue.

4 If your metal letter has a loop at the top, use wire cutters to snip it off. Hot-glue the metal letter to the lower right corner of the card. Glue the three tiny rhinestones along the left edge of the letter.

Crystal Satin Guest Book

Glimmering discreetly, crystal sliders create gentle tufts in the padded satin cover of this guest book. A simple monogram rests on a band of pearl-edged ribbon, but there's room for up to three initials if you desire.

How To Make It

Materials

Purchased guest book, 6 x 8 inches

Quilt batting, 8 x 18 inches

Spray adhesive

Satin fabric, 10 x 20 inches

1 yard of satin ribbon, 1/8 inch wide

Beading thread

6 Swarovski crystal sliders

2 sheets of silver card stock, 8 1/2 x 11 inches

1 1/4 yards of cream-colored pearl-edged ribbon, 1 inch wide

Metal monogram with loop

Pearl bead, 4mm

Matching thread

Tools & Supplies

Tape measure

Scissors (both paper and fabric)

Iron and ironing board

Ruler and pencil

Hot glue and glue gun

6-inch upholstery needle

Large-eye embroidery needle

Glue stick

Sewing needle

Designer: Joan K. Morris

1 Find the center page of the guest book. Place the open book on a flat surface with the covers facing up. Cut the quilt batting to the exact size of the open guest book. Use the spray adhesive to attach the batting to the covers and spine.

2 Iron the satin, and cut it to the size of the open guest book plus 1 inch all the way around. Place the satin right side down on a flat surface. Center the open guest book, covers side down, on top.

3 You'll now start to hot-glue the excess satin to the inside of the covers; in order to accommodate the spine, it works best to start at the short edges of the book. Hot-glue the 1-inch excess at each short edge to the inside of the covers, keeping the fabric tight, but not so tight that the book can't open and close easily.

4 Open the book at its center and place it paper side down. At the top and bottom of the spine, cut two 1-inch-deep slits 1/2 inch apart to leave a piece of satin to push into the spine, but leave these unglued for now. Hot-glue the long edges down at the top and bottom, pulling tightly. When the edges are done, place a dab of hot glue on each piece at the spine and push them into the spine.

5 Thread the upholstery needle with the 1/8-inch ribbon. Run the needle and ribbon up through the spine, and tie a small bow with long tails.

6 Thread the embroidery needle with the beading thread. Decide where you want to

place the crystal sliders. To tuft for the crystals, start from the inside front cover of the book, push the needle through to the top and then back down to the inside. Pull tightly and knot.

7 Hot-glue the crystal sliders in place.

8 Cut the silver card stock to the exact size of the inside front cover of the guest book. Adhere the card stock to the inside cover by coating the entire back with the glue stick,

placing the card stock on the inside cover, and carefully rubbing out any air pockets or wrinkles. Repeat this procedure to add silver card stock to the inside back cover.

9 Cut three 14-inch-long pieces of the pearl-edged ribbon. Fold over one end of each ribbon, and hot-glue the fold to create a hem.

10 Place the unhemmed end of one ribbon in the center of the inside front cover. Hot-glue

the unhemmed end of the ribbon in place, wrap the ribbon around to the front cover, and then hand-stitch the metal monogram and the pearl to the front of the ribbon, referring to the photo for placement. Now wrap the hemmed end of the ribbon back around to the inside front cover, and hot-glue it over the unhemmed end.

11 Add the other two ribbons to either side of the middle one, following the method described in step 10.

Monogrammed Accordion Photo Album

Share moments of your wedding day with your bridal party by presenting each member with this chic photo album. Consider personalizing each album by including photos that will have special meaning to them.

Materials

Sheet of floral embossed
 scrapbooking paper, 12 x 12 inches

4 sheets of card stock,
 12 x 12 inches

1½ yards of ribbon printed
 with words

Chipboard (or cardboard)

¼ yard of stranded mini pearls

Metal monogram

Silk blossoms, assorted sizes

Miniature rhinestones

2 metal photo corners

Tools & Supplies

Scissors or paper trimmer

Glue stick

Hole punch

Wire cutters

Hot glue and glue gun

Designer: Brandy Logan

How To Make It

1 Cut two 5 x 7-inch pieces of the floral embossed paper and six 5 x 7-inch pieces of the card stock.

2 Attach one 5 x 7-inch card stock piece to the back of each

5 x 7-inch embossed piece using a glue stick. You now have the front and back covers of the album.

3 Place the two embossed sheets back to back, and punch

two evenly spaced holes along the left edge.

4 Take the four remaining pieces of card stock, and using an already-punched embossed piece as a guide, punch two matching holes on the left side of each piece. Turn one piece of punched card stock over, and use it to make two holes on the right side of each of the four pieces of cardstock. You should now have four pieces of cardstock with holes on both sides.

5 Next you'll tie these four pieces of cardstock together into one long strip that folds accordion-style. To begin, cut the worded ribbon into eight 5-inch pieces. Line up the four card stock pieces into one long horizontal strip. Tie each piece to the one next to it using a 5-inch piece of ribbon. Knot the ribbon for each "hinge," and cut the ends short. Save the two unused 5-inch lengths of ribbon.

6 Cut a 10-inch strand of the worded ribbon in half, making sure each half has two words. Use these strands of ribbon to tie one end of the accordion strip to the front cover. Tie each strand with a simple knot in the front of the cover, leaving the ends long and arranging the ribbon so the words can be read. Tie the other end of the accordion strip to the back cover using the two remaining 5-inch lengths of ribbon. Cut the ribbon ends short.

7 You'll now add card stock-covered chipboard pieces to the covers to provide both stability and a colored border. To begin, cut the chipboard into two 5 x 7¼-inch pieces. (These pieces are slightly higher than the covers so they'll show when placed behind them.) Cover each chipboard piece entirely with the card stock using a glue stick.

8 Place one piece behind the front cover, arranged so its left edge is about ¼ inch in from the spine. You have it positioned correctly when it creates about a ⅛-inch border on the top, bottom, and right sides of the embossed cover. Mark this position on the back of the cover with a pencil if needed, and then attach it to the cover using a glue stick.

Repeat this procedure to attach the remaining chipboard piece to the back cover.

9 Run a strand of mini pearls through the front cover's holes, and tie in place.

10 If your metal letter has a loop at the top, use wire cutters to snip it off. Cut a 2 x 2-inch square of card stock, and adhere a metal monogram in the center using a glue stick. Glue the monogrammed square on the center of the front cover with the glue stick.

11 Using the hot glue gun, attach the blossoms around the monogrammed square, overlapping them for a full look. Attach miniature rhinestones into the centers of the blossoms using a small dab of hot glue.

12 Adhere the metal photo corners to the front cover's right corners with hot glue.

The Origin of the Word Honeymoon

One of the sweetest accounts of the origin of the word honeymoon is derived from the honey-based wine known as mead. According to many sources, there was a custom in ancient northern European times whereby the newly married couple was supplied with enough of this honeyed wine for a month—one moon. This, it was believed, would enhance fertility, especially for a son.

Happily Ever After
Scrapbook Page

Your wedding was flawless—down to the smallest detail. Once you've caught your breath, take a moment to organize your photos while the details of the day are fresh in your mind. This scrapbook page provides you with a spot to place a poem, quote, or your own thoughts.

Once in a while, right in the middle of an ordinary life, love gives us a fairy tale.

Materials

Sheet of diamond-patterned
paper, 12 x 12 inches

2 sheets of card stock,
12 x 12 inches

Adhesive tabs

Focal photo

Sheet of floral embossed paper,
12 x 12 inches

24 inches of stranded mini pearls

Beaded word "LOVE"

3 silk blossoms

3 pearl beads

Sheet of clear vellum,
8-1/2 x 11 inches

6 inches of pearl-edged ribbon

Tools & Supplies

Scissors or paper trimmer

Ruler

Paper adhesive

Computer and printer

Hole punch

How To Make It

1 Cut a 3 x 12-inch strip of
the diamond-patterned paper.
Mount the strip across the top
of one sheet of the cream-colored card stock (your background sheet), about 3/4 inch
down from the top.

2 Cut one sheet of cream-colored card stock into a rectangle
that's 1/2 inch larger than the
photo on all sides. Cut the floral embossed paper into a rectangle that's about 1/2 inch larger
than the card stock rectangle.
Double mat the photo on the
cream-colored and the floral
embossed paper.

3 Mount the photo on the
right side of the layout, being
sure to overlap the diamond-
patterned strip (use the project
photo for reference).

4 Cut a 12-inch strand of mini
pearls, and glue it to the top
edge of the diamond-patterned
strip. Measure and cut two
strands to fit across the bottom
of the diamond-patterned strip,
on either side of the mounted
photo. Glue these in place.

5 Glue the beaded word
"LOVE" to the diamond-patterned strip, to the left of the
mounted photo.

6 Glue two blossoms onto the
upper right corner of the photo
and one blossom to the lower
left corner. Glue a pearl bead
into the center of each blossom.

7 Cut a 1 x 12-inch strip of
the diamond paper, and horizontally mount it across the
bottom of the layout, 1 inch up
from the bottom.

8 Print your message onto the
vellum, and then cut around the
text to create a rectangle. Cut
the floral embossed paper into a
rectangle slightly larger than the
vellum rectangle.

9 To create the holes to attach
the ribbon, carefully position
the vellum over the silver rectangle, and then punch two
holes through both sheets, centered at the top and about 1
inch apart.

10 Make the bow by first
threading each end of the
pearl-edged ribbon through the
holes from the front side of the
card to the back. Cross the ribbon ends on the back side of
the card, and then pull each
through the opposite side's
hole. Tighten the bow and trim
each end with a diagonal cut.
Glue this to the lower left side
of the layout.

Designer: Brandy Logan

Rice Toss Tin

Cut a length of wired ribbon and fold it over at a right angle in the middle. Twist a jeweled wire wedding embellishment around two wedding rings and then around the ribbon center. Hot-glue the folded ribbon to the top of the tin. Fill the tin with rice, birdseed, or confetti. Curl the ribbon ends.

Designer: Linda Kopp

Ribbon-Wrapped Votive

Wrap a wide ribbon around the center of a votive and hot-glue in place. Center a narrower length of ribbon over the wider ribbon and hot-glue. Set on a small silver tray.

Designer: Terry Taylor

Fabric Frame Favor

Hot-glue a wedding ring and jeweled wedding embellishment to a fabric frame. Insert photograph.

Designer: Terry Taylor

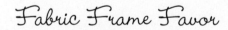

Wedding Program

Following the manufacturer's instructions, use a computer to type the program wording, and print it out. Thread two wedding rings onto ribbon. Wrap the ribbon around the folded program, overlap, and glue the ends together.

Designer: *Linda Kopp*

Keepsake Chest

Purchase a premade fabric-covered chest. Remove any embellishments except for the trim. Hot-glue silk flowers on the lid using two flower varieties. Make small loops out of ribbon, gluing the loose ends together. Glue them amongst the flowers, using the photo as a guide. Create a longer ribbon loop and glue to the front of the chest. Cover the ends with smaller ribbon loops and silk flowers.

Designer: *Linda Kopp*

Pretty in Pink

Every bride by definition is romantic...but some have a touch more romance than most. They're the women who've dreamed of their wedding day forever—the ones who, as little girls, wore lacy pink dresses and insisted on matching satin bows in their hair; who dressed their dolls as brides and who, as teenagers, poured through bridal magazines to find the perfect dress and fantasized about their boyfriends on bended knee, asking for their hand.

To many, pink is the time-chosen color of romance. From the color in the blush of a maid's cheek when her suitor is close, to the soft, pink shades of dew-ladened roses, pink reigns the realm of love. The look is timeless, lovely... and as romantic as you'll feel walking down that aisle.

Pearl-Entwined Rose Bridal Bouquet

Worldwide, the rose has long been the symbol of undying love. This cluster of roses is adorned with tiny strands of pearls and a luxurious white-on-white fabric bow.

How To Make It

Materials

7 large silk roses

Plastic bouquet holder with poly-styrene insert

2 packages of 26-gauge 18-inch white cloth-covered stem wire

3 packages of pearls on monofila-ment, 18-inch strands (9 strands per package)

White floral tape

50 pearl-headed corsage pins

3 yards of wired brocade ribbon, 2½ inches wide

Tools & Supplies

Scissors

Ruler

Wire cutters

Designer: Joan K. Morris

1 Cut the stems of the roses to 4 inches long. Place one rose in the center top of the bou-quet holder. Evenly space the rest of the roses around the center rose, being careful to close up any gaps.

2 Twist three 18-inch cloth-covered wires together at one end. Braid the three wires together and twist the other ends together. Repeat until you have a total of nine braided wires.

3 Form a pretzel-shaped loop from one of the braided wires. Bring the two loops in from either end to the center where the wires cross. Twist the wires together under the center. Repeat with the remain-ing eight braided wires.

4 Place three of the pearl monofilament strands together. Place one of the ends at the bottom of one of the pretzels where it's twisted together. Wrap a small piece of white flo-ral tape around the ends to hold in position. Wrap the pearl monofilament from one loop to the next until complete. Wrap the ends with more floral tape. Repeat on the remaining eight braided wires.

5 At the base of the plastic bouquet holder, place one set of pearl-wrapped loops under the roses. Attach it to the poly-styrene base by running a pearl-

ribbon down one side of the plastic and up the other, securing with corsage pins every few inches. You will have formed a "U" shape of ribbon on either side of the handle.

8 When the ribbon meets where you started, wrap the ribbon in a spiral manner down the handle, then halfway back up. Cut. Fold the end of the ribbon under and secure with a corsage pin.

9 To make the bow, center the remaining ribbon in the upper back of the handle and pin in place. Bring ends to the front and tie into a bow. Leave about a 15-inch trail of ribbon. Cut the ends at an angle.

headed corsage pin through the twisted center bottom and then into the polystyrene. Place one pearl-headed corsage pin on either side of the center through the braiding of the wire to secure.

6 Repeat with the remaining eight pieces, overlapping each successive piece, and securing

with corsage pins until the roses are fully encircled.

7 Wrap the handle with ribbon by taking the end of the ribbon and placing it with the long edge under the roses at the top of the plastic. Place a corsage pin through the ribbon into the polystyrene. Lay the

Scalloped Heart Invitation

Classic and stylish elegance is the message that will surround your wedding invitation with this romantic presentation. The scalloped window in this invitation frames a heart of roses, drawing the recipient inside to share the who, what, when, and where of your special day.

Materials

One premade tri-fold card with scalloped window opening and plain window on second flap (5 x 7-inch folded size)

Sheet of toile patterned paper, 8½ x 11 inches

Sheet of solid color pearlized/metallic paper, 8½ x 11 inches

Sheet of ivory card stock to match the card, 8½ x 11 inches

Gold pigment ink

Gold embossing powder

Sheet of pink and gold floral-patterned paper

18 inches of pink tulle, 6 inches wide

Tools & Supplies

Paper trimmer

Pencil

Glue stick

Craft knife

Large rubber heart-shaped wreath stamp

Heat embossing tool

Light pink marker

Cotton swab

Computer and printer

1 Using a paper trimmer, cut a 5 x 7-inch rectangle of toile paper. Place facedown on a work surface. Place the front cover of the card facedown on top of the back side of the toile paper. Trace the scalloped window with a pencil onto the paper. Draw a window ¼-inch larger than the scalloped window; cut with a craft knife. Glue the toile paper to the cover flap.

2 Cut a 5 x 7-inch rectangle of pearlized/metallic solid colored paper and place it facedown. Place the second flap of the card facedown on top of the back side of the solid paper. Trace the window and cut it out. Glue the solid paper onto the second flap.

3 Cut a 2¼-inch square out of the ivory card stock. Stamp a heart-shaped wreath, using gold ink, onto the center of the square. Sprinkle with gold embossing powder. Use the embossing tool to heat set (see page 173 for more on embossing). Color in the image with the pink marker. Glue the square over the window so that the heart faces out.

4 Cut a 5 x 7-inch rectangle of floral-patterned paper. Fold each side in ¼ inch. Wet each crease with a cotton swab, tear to create a ragged edge, then glue it to the inside center panel.

Together with their families

Ashley Elaine

and

Grayson S. Olson

invite you to share in the joy
and celebration of their marriage
on Saturday, the fifth of August
two thousand and six
at two o'clock in the afternoon
Trinity Baptist Church
126 Howell Mill Rd.
Trinity, North Carolina 27370

5 Making sure to stay within a 2½ x 4¼ inch area, type the invitation wording onto the ivory card stock and print it out. Trim to 3¼ x 4 ¾ inches. Glue the wording onto the metallic paper. Measure and cut the metallic paper ⅛-inch larger than the printed card stock to create a border trim. Center and glue onto the patterned paper.

6 Repeat step 3 to make a second stamped image. In addition, scrape the paper's edges against the gold ink, sprinkle with gold embossing powder and then heat set. Glue the card stock to the inside right panel to cover the back side of the first stamped image.

7 Wrap the tulle around the left flap and tie into a knot. Trim the ends.

Designer: Brandy Logan

Dreamy Swagged Cake

On first glance, your guests may find it hard to believe that this cake is decorated with bows and draped with swags made of fondant instead of fabric. The lacy designs are actually stenciled with icing.

Materials

Three cake layers:

12-inch round cake, 4 inches tall

10-inch round cake, 4 inches tall

8-inch round cake, 4 inches tall

Buttercream icing (see recipe on page 193)

Round cake board, 16 x 1-inch board

Gold wrapping paper

48 ounces of white fondant (for 12-inch layer)

36 ounces of white fondant (for 10-inch layer)

24 ounces of white fondant (for 8-inch layer)

Confectioner's sugar

Wooden dowel, ¼-inch diameter

Cake board, 10-inch diameter

Cake board, 8-inch diameter

Lace stencil

White ready-to-use icing in a tube (with built-in tip)

24 ounces of white fondant (for swags and bows)

4 large silk roses

Eighteen 18-inch white fabric-covered wires, 26-gauge

2 packages of pearl and monofilament, 18 inches long

Pearl-headed floral pins

Designer: Joan K. Morris

Tools & Supplies

Cake leveler or serrated knife

Cake decorating turntable

Large angled spatula

Scissors

Cellophane tape

Gridded roll and cut cake mat

Large rolling pin

Fondant smoothing tool

Poly blade cutter or craft knife

Ruler

Small rolling pin

Wire cutters

How To Make It

Covering the Cake Board & Stacking the Cake

1 Follow the cake instructions, and bake. Cool, and level. Ice the cake layers with buttercream icing (see pages 178–180).

2 Cover the 16-inch cake board with gold wrapping paper by cutting out a circle of wrapping paper 3 inches larger than the cake board. Set the cake board circle in the center of the wrong side of the wrapping paper. Wrap the paper over the edge and to the back, creasing the edge to make it fit. Tape in place.

3 Cover the cake layers with fondant (see pages 180–181).

4 Stack the cake layers (refer to pages 183–184). Let sit for an hour.

Applying the Icing Stencil

5 Decide what portion of the stencil you want to use on the sides of the cake, and cut it out.

6 Place about a teaspoon of ready-to-use icing onto a plate. Hold the stencil in position on the cake. Using the spatula, pick up some of the icing and place it on the stencil. Push the icing into the stencil with the spatula and then wipe it across, leaving a small amount of icing in the stencil. Carefully remove

Cakes for Less

For brides on a budget, a beautiful wedding cake may seem out of the question. But, with a few cost-friendly suggestions, you can have your cake and eat it too. If you have your heart set on a many-tiered masterpiece but can't handle the towering price of one, polystyrene foam blocks can be iced and used for some of the tiers of the cake. No one will ever be the wiser.

One trend that has become popular at celebrity weddings is to have a small centerpiece cake at each table. This is a novel and effective way to tailor the cost of a wedding cake to the needs of your guests and create a centerpiece at the same time.

Cupcake wedding cakes are another innovative option, costing much less than a traditional cake. Cupcakes in a variety of flavors can be decorated and stacked to create an endless variety of designs.

Don't forget to tap into the talents of family members. Perhaps one relative could bake the cakes, while another assembles and decorates the layers.

the stencil. If you're not happy with the way it looks, scrape the icing off and try again. Repeat this all the way around the layers.

Making & Attaching the Fondant Decorations

7 On the top layer, measure out five evenly spaced spots on the edge. Mark them with a small slice using the poly blade cutter or craft knife. This is where you will place the bows.

8 To make the bows, roll out a ⅛-inch-thick piece of fondant to measure about 5 x 7 inches. Cut ½-inch-wide strips of fondant. From those strips cut three 3-inch-long pieces and two 2-inch-long pieces. Fold two of the 3-inch-long pieces in half and pinch the ends together like the center of a bow. Take the other 3-inch piece and place it vertically in front of you. Place the pinched ends of the other two on the lower end. Bring the upper end over the pinched pieces and wrap around, creating the center of the bow. Take the 2-inch pieces and cut one end of each at an angle. Place the flat ends under the bow to look like the ends of a ribbon bow. See additional technique instructions on page 188.

9 Place the bow on the upper edge of the top layer on one of the marks by applying a line of ready-to-use icing around the underside of the bow (the icing acts like glue).

10 Repeat the process for the other four marks on the top edge of the top layer.

11 To make the swags, roll out fondant to ⅛ inch thick. Cut out a piece 2½ x 5 inches. Pinch the 2½-inch sides together from top to bottom. Make two rows of folds by shaping the fondant with your hands. See pages 188–189 for additional technique instructions.

12 Hold the swag up between two of the bows to see if it needs to be cut to fit. If needed, cut the pinched ends to the correct length. Place a line of icing on the back of the swag, making sure to put a dab at each end. Place the swag in position and lightly push it in place next to the bows. If it starts to slip, hold it in position for a minute. If it's humid or hot, the fondant may sag, so try to work in a cool area. It will stay in position once it's dry.

13 Repeat steps 6 through 12 on the two lower layers, lining up the five bows below the top bows. The only difference is the bows should be cut ¾ inch wide.

14 Roll out pea-sized balls of fondant and line them up side by side all the way around the base of each layer. Secure them with a dab of ready-to-use icing under each.

Creating the Topper

15 Cut the stems of the roses, leaving 2 inches of stem under each flower. Evenly space the roses on the top of the cake and push in the stems. This is enough to hold them in place.

16 Line up three of the 18-inch fabric-covered wires and three of the pearl-and-monofilament pieces. Twist one of the wire ends around the rest to hold them all together. Place a monofilament piece with each wire, and braid all of them together. Repeat this step until you have six braided pieces.

17 Cut the braided pieces in half using the wire cutters. Bend each piece to form an oval and twist the ends together.

18 To hold the braided strands in place, push the pearl-headed pins through the bottom of the strands near the twisted end, and into the cake.

Fondant-Decorated Shortbread Cookies

These cookies are as much a delight to the eyes as to the taste buds. The fondant adds an elegant touch to your favorite shortbread or sugar cookie recipe, and the design possibilities are endless— limited only by your imagination.

Materials

Cookie dough

Pre-tinted fondant
(or white fondant and
concentrated icing color)

White fondant

Thinned fondant adhesive
(optional, see page 193
for recipe)

Royal icing
(see recipe on page 96)

Tools & Supplies

Rolling pin

Roll and cut mat

Cornstarch

Cookie cutters in desired shapes

Spatula

Fondant ribbon cutter/embosser

Pastry bag with coupler and a
#2 tip, or a clean, empty squeeze
bottle with a small tip

How To Make It

1 Prepare a rolled cookie dough that will result in a cookie that is firm, flat, and smooth—a shortbread or sugar cookie recipe works nicely.

2 Use various cookie cutters and cut out the desired shapes. Bake according to the recipe and cool thoroughly.

3 Refer to page 184 and tint fondant to the desired color, or use pre-tinted, ready-to-use fondant (available in a variety of colors). To cover a cookie in fondant, lightly dust a roll and cut mat with cornstarch, and roll the colored fondant out to a 1/8-inch thickness.

4 For the base cookie covering, use the same cutter shape as the cookie you wish to place it on. Press the cutter firmly through the fondant. Remove any excess fondant from around the edges, lift the cut shape with a spatula, and position it on the cookie. For thicker baked goods, like the square one shown in the photo, cut a fondant square large enough to cover the sides.

Designer: Chris Rankin

or with thinned fondant adhesive.

6 Create the decorative strips with a fondant ribbon cutter/embosser, following the manufacturer's instructions. Attach them as described in Step 5. To achieve an "inlay" look, review page 187.

5 Following Step 3, roll out a few ounces of white fondant. Make smaller fondant decorations with different cutter shapes. Using the project photograph as a guide for placement, attach the shapes by brushing the backs with water

7 Pipe white dots using royal icing in the pastry bag or squeeze bottle.

Cookie Recipies

Shortbread Cookies

Ingredients

1 cup butter

1/2 cup granulated sugar

2 tsp vanilla extract

3 large egg yolks

2 1/2 cups sifted cake flour

Instructions

1. Cream the butter, sugar, and vanilla extract.

2. Blend in the egg yolks.

3. Add the flour, mixing only until combined.

4. Refrigerate to set. Keep the dough wrapped to avoid drying the surface.

5. Bake at 350°F for 10-12 minutes

Sugar Cookies

Ingredients

1 cup butter

1/2 cup granulated sugar

2 tsp vanilla extract

1 beaten egg

2 1/2 cups all-purpose flour

Instructions

1. Cream the butter, sugar, and vanilla extract.

2. Blend in the beaten egg.

3. Add the flour, mixing only until combined.

4. Refrigerate to set. Keep the dough wrapped to avoid drying the surface.

5. Bake at 350°F for 10-12 minutes

Bridesmaid Treasure Box

What better place for your bridesmaid to store something beloved than a hand-decorated box from a dear friend—you? This mini-chest makes a wonderful place for her to tuck away a cherished possession, whether it's a dried flower from someone special, or a favorite pair of earrings.

Materials

Wooden box with hinged lid,
5½ x 3 x 3 inches

White craft paint

Colored craft paint

Stencil

Colored dimensional paint

White pearl craft paint

High gloss clear coat spray

¼ yard of white satin

Tools & Supplies

Phillips-head screwdriver

Sandpaper, medium grit

Paintbrush, 1 inch wide

Masking tape

Spray adhesive

Small putty knife

Scissors

Iron and ironing board

Hot glue and glue gun

Designer: Joan K. Morris

How To Make It

1 Remove the lid from the wooden box by unscrewing the hinges. Remove the latch hardware.

2 Sand the wooden box and lid.

3 Paint the box with white craft paint. Paint the lid with colored craft paint. Let them dry.

4 Decide where you want to place the designs on the box. If there are any areas in the stencil that you don't want to come through, cover them with masking tape. You will need to place the dimensional paint on one side at a time and let each side dry before moving to the next side.

5 Lightly spray the wrong side of the stencil with spray adhesive, and position it on the box. Following the manufacturer's instructions, place a dab of the colored dimensional paint on the stencil using the putty knife, then spread the paint over the stencil. Carefully remove the stencil by lifting from one end and pulling it off. Clean the stencil. Let the dimensional paint dry. This may take several hours. Repeat this step around the rest of the box.

6 Bend the stencil over the edge of the lid, and put the dimensional paint on in one step. If the spray adhesive doesn't hold the stencil down, hold the area you're working on down with one hand while spreading the dimensional paint with the other. Carefully remove the stencil. Let dry.

7 When all the paint has dried, paint the box and lid with a thin coat of the white pearl paint. Once dry, lightly sand the dimensional area to expose some of the color. Let dry.

8 Spray the box and the lid with three coats of gloss clear coat spray, letting the coats dry between applications.

9 Cut a 9 x 12-inch piece of white satin. Fold and press a ½-inch hem all the way around the edges of the satin.

10 To line the box, place a dab of hot glue in the center of the bottom of the box, and place the satin inside, pressing the center of the satin piece into the glue. Arrange the satin, leaving it loose and billowy. Glue the edges down by dabbing glue inside the box and placing the fabric all the way around the inside of the box, making sure the lid has room to close.

Double-Duty Menu/Place Card

It's a place card—no wait—a pretty holder for a menu. Actually, it serves both functions quite nicely. This clever two-in-one project not only guides your guests to their seats, but also informs them as to what culinary delights await.

Menu

Appetizer
-hot artichoke dip with pita triangles

Soup and Salad
-French onion soup in a sourdough bread boule
-Field greens served with house dressing

Entree
-Prime rib roast served with au jus
-Garlic mashed potatoes
-Sautéed spinach

Dessert
-Lemon wedding cake with buttercream icing

---Open Bar---

Mrs. Tracy Ducker

Materials

Card stock

Brown ink pad

Decorative brad

Floral scrapbooking paper

18 inches of sheer ribbon,
  ½ inch wide

Tools & Supplies

Computer and printer

Tag template (available at craft
  supply stores)

Pencil

Scissors or paper trimmer

Glue stick

Designer: Brandy Logan

How To Make It

1 Choose a computer font you like, and then type and print your menu onto the card stock, setting the margins so the text will fit an area the size of the tag template. Type and print your guest's name onto the card stock (make certain the name isn't wider than the tag's width). Place the template over the menu, trace, and cut out.

2 "Antique" the tag's edges by brushing them lightly over the top of the brown ink pad. When the ink has dried, insert the decorative brad into the top of the tag.

3 To begin making the envelope, cut the floral paper into a strip about ½ inch wider than the tag and a little longer than twice the tag's length. Fold this paper in half lengthwise.

4 Using the tag template as a guide, trim the top of the folded strip so the tag's top will just show when placed inside. Unfold the strip of paper and set it pattern-side-down on a flat surface. Fold each of the side edges in about ¼ inch. Fold the strip back in half lengthwise to form an envelope, and use a glue stick to secure the sides.

5 Cut the name from the cream-colored card stock to form a small rectangle. "Antique" the edges of the floral envelope and the name tag by brushing them lightly across the top of the brown ink pad. Attach the name tag to the bottom of the envelope.

6 Finish by tying a ribbon around the envelope. Trim the ribbon ends by folding them in half and cutting at a 45° angle.

When I was young, I dreamed
of finding someone really special
who would come into my life
and love me wholly and uniquely...
someone who would understand my desires,
encourage my efforts, and share my dreams...

When I grew older
I found that person;
I love you for loving me just the way
I dreamed it would be. - Unknown

Sarah Louise Johnson
May 24th, 2004
Salt Lake City, Utah

Cherish

Gold-Trimmed Scrapbook Page

Gilded pearls, beaded fabric flowers, and soft tulle (pink, of course!) create an utterly feminine page. Consider using a black and white photo to add a striking look.

Materials

Sheet of patterned paper, 12 x 12-inches

Sheet of cream-colored card stock, 12 x 12 inches

Adhesive tabs

Sheet of script-patterned vellum, 12 x 12 inches

Vertical photo

Sheet of gold paper, 12 x 12 inches

Sheet of coordinating patterned paper, 12 x 12 inches

1 yard of tulle, 4 inches wide

Temporary tape

2 sheets of cream-colored card stock, 8½ x 11 inches

4 eyelets

1 yard of ribbon, ½-inch wide

6 brads

Printer-ready acetate (optional, see step 8)

12 inches of stranded mini-pearls

3 silk flowers with pearls

4 photo corners

Tools & Supplies

Scissors or paper trimmer

Ruler or straightedge

Paper glue

Sewing machine and thread

Computer and printer

Gold-leaf pen

Photocopier (optional, see step 8)

Designer: Trudy Sigurdson

How To Make It

1 Trim one sheet of patterned paper to 11 x 11 inches and mount it on the center of the 12 x 12-inch sheet of cream-colored card stock. Place the sheet of script-patterned vellum over these two papers. Adhere the vellum to the background in places that will eventually be covered by other elements, such as the photo—not in places where the adhesive will show through the vellum.

2 Cut a strip of gold paper, and mount it horizontally to the bottom of the sheet of vellum, aligning the bottom and sides. Cut a slightly narrower strip of the coordinating patterned paper and mount it horizontally on top of the gold paper.

3 Cut the tulle into two 14-inch-long strands. Gather the strands and wrap them across the top and bottom of the page, adhering the ends to the back with temporary tape. (We made our bottom strand slightly wider than the top one.)

4 Machine-stitch around all sides of this assembly; then

stitch across the top of the patterned strip at the bottom of the page.

5 Mat your photo on a rectangle of gold paper, and adhere it to the left side of the page, tilting it slightly to the left. The photo should overlap the tulle at the top of the page and the gold and patterned papers at the bottom.

Adding a Gold-Leaf Border

Purchase a gold-leaf pen with a chisel tip, and you should be able to "hook" the tip onto the edge of your paper and draw a nice straight gold border. Practice a few times on scrap paper first. An alternative is to simply use a straight-edge or ruler to guide you as you draw around the edge of your paper.

6 Print your text onto the cream-colored card stock; then cut around it to form three rectangles. Outline the edges of each rectangle with the gold-leaf pen.

7 Attach eyelets to these text blocks and tie each with a short length of ribbon. Attach the text blocks to the page with brads on one side. Further secure the text blocks with adhesive squares.

8 The word "cherish" was printed in a very large typeface onto card stock that was cut out and painted with the gold-leaf pen. Because you'll need to paint the side without ink, reverse your word before printing it if you have a computer program that will do so. Otherwise, first print the word onto a sheet of clear printer-ready acetate, and then position the acetate onto a photocopier so the word will come

out in reverse when it's copied. Carefully cut out the letters and color them with the gold-leaf pen. Tie a ribbon around the extender of one letter before using the liquid scrapbooking glue to attach the letters to the page (see the project photo for placement).

9 Use the liquid glue to attach the stranded pearls to the bottom strand of tulle. If desired, use the gold-leaf pen to color some of the pearls first.

10 Embellish the flowers with ribbon, and then attach them to the page with the liquid glue. Before gluing the two flowers to the tulle on the bottom, gather the tulle by tying thread around it.

11 Use the gold-leaf pen to add a thin gold border to the entire page and then attach the gold photo corners.

Gilded Frame Shadowbox

Protect and display your most prized wedding memorabilia in a framed shadowbox. The gilded frame worthy of any masterpiece sets a romantic tone.

Materials

Shadowbox with hinged glass front, 14 x 18 inches

Decorative frame, 14 x 18 inches

Gold spray paint

Rub-on gold wax

Patterned scrapbook paper

Tools & Supplies

Sandpaper, medium grit

Masking tape

Paintbrush, 1 inch wide

Thin artist brush

Scissors

Glue stick

Drill and $3/32$ drill bit

4 wood screws, $1^{1}/4$ inches

Screwdriver

6 finish nails, 1 inch long

Hammer

White craft glue

Designer: *Joan K. Morris*

Crossing the Threshold

When we speak of being "swept off our feet" we usually mean that we're madly in love. The term, however, did not always carry this connotation of love and affection. Now seen as a romantic gesture, the tradition of carrying a bride over the threshold has come a long way from its origins. In recent past, it was linked to female modesty. Women were expected to appear hesitant in consenting to enter the bridal chamber, prompting their husbands to pick them up and carry them in.

Superstition played its part in the birth of this ritual. Ancient beliefs claimed that newlyweds were very susceptible to bad luck and harm. Some claimed that evil spirits lay in wait under the threshold—carrying a bride over the threshold would keep her safe from them. Some old beliefs also held that a bride tripping or stumbling across the threshold would bring bad luck to the marriage. To eliminate this danger, the husband would carry her. Early roots of the tradition also date back to a time when brides were captured by enemy tribes and forced into marriage. Under such circumstances, a bride was seldom cooperative in entering the bridal chamber and therefore had to be carried or dragged.

How To Make It

1 Remove the back of the shadowbox and the shelf.

2 Lightly sand the shadowbox and frame.

3 Place masking tape where the glass meets the wood on the inside and outside of the shadowbox door. Use the 1-inch paintbrush to paint the shadowbox white. Use the artist brush to paint in tight spaces and around the hinges. Apply two or three coats.

4 Spray-paint the frame gold. Let dry.

5 Paint over the gold with white craft paint. Let dry. Lightly sand over the raised areas on the frame to let the gold color show through. Sand areas that would normally show wear to give the frame an aged appearance. To add more gold, rub your finger in the gold wax, and then on the raised areas of the frame.

6 Using the glue stick, cover the entire backboard and shelf with the scrapbooking paper.

If you must use two sheets of paper to cover the backboard, try to place the seam where the two sheets join behind the shelf.

7 Center the frame on the front of the shadowbox. Holding the frame in place, turn the shadowbox over. Mark four spots on the back of the shadowbox frame, two on each side. Drill the marked areas about $\frac{1}{2}$ inch deep. Place a screw in each hole and tighten with the screwdriver.

8 Return the backboard to its original place on the back of the shadowbox. Hammer six finish nails into the edge of the shadowbox over the board, leaving $\frac{1}{2}$ inch of the nails sticking out over the board. Place two nails on each vertical side edge, and one each in both the top and bottom edges.

9 Place the shelf in position.

Satin Flower Girl Basket

This flower girl basket is as dainty as the little girl you select to fill the role—and after the petals have been strewn, it makes a pretty keepsake that she will love.

Materials

Satin flower girl basket

1 1/3 yards of wired fabric ribbon, 2 1/2 inches wide

Silk peonies

12 inches of narrow gold ribbon

Rose petals (we used silk)

Tools & Supplies

Scissors

Floral wire

Hot glue and glue gun

Designer: Linda Kopp

How To Make It

1 Twist a length of fabric ribbon to fashion three loops, leaving enough ribbon on each end to form streamers. Use floral wire to hold the loops in place, and then wire the loops to the basket handle.

2 Loosely drape another piece of ribbon up one side of the handle and down the other, gently twisting the ribbon to produce a soft, flowing look.

3 Use the wire stems of the silk peonies to attach them to the handle, using the project picture as a guide for placement.

4 Hot-glue a length of gold ribbon around the bottom of the basket.

Tip

Fill your basket with silk, dried, or natural flower petals.

Embellished Guest Book

When planning your wedding, consider taking ready-made items and personalizing them to match your wedding theme. With a touch of ribbon, a bit of fabric, and a dash from a watercolor pencil, this guest book can quickly mirror the color palette of any wedding.

Materials

Pre-made guest book with cake
 design insert

2 watercolor pencils

2 sheets of patterned scrapbooking
 paper, 8½ x 11 inches

2 yards of braided ribbon,
 ⅛ inch wide

1 yard of mesh ribbon, ½ inch wide

Tools & Supplies

Scrap piece of paper

Thin artist paintbrush

Ruler

Pencil

Scissors

Glue stick

Hot glue and glue gun

Designer: Joan K. Morris

How To Make It

1 Remove the raffia that holds the book together. Take off the front and back covers, keeping the inside pages together.

2 Practice using the water-color pencils on a scrap piece of paper. Lightly color a small area of the paper, then dip the paintbrush in water and stroke over the colored area. You will see it blend and change color. You want to achieve a washed look. Place more color with the pencils and apply more water with the paintbrush until you get the desired result. If the color looks too dark, just add more water and spread the color out. Leave some areas without color.

3 Once you feel comfortable with the technique, you are ready to start working on the back cover of the book. For a nice overall look, place the colors in a diagonal direction, from the upper-right corner to the lower-left corner. Work on the front in the same way.

4 On the cake insert, draw on the flower petal with the water-color pencils and add water.

5 Measure the inside covers of the guest book and transfer those measurements to the sheets of decorative paper, making sure the design of the paper is facing the correct direction. Cut them out.

6 Using the glue stick, apply a coat of glue to the back of the paper, and place it on the inside cover. Rub out any trapped air bubbles. Repeat the process for the inside back cover.

7 Cut a piece of ⅛-inch-wide braided ribbon to go around the edge of the paper. Run a thin, 2-inch-long line of hot glue on the edge of the paper. Place the end of the ribbon on this line of glue, being careful not to burn your fingers on the glue. Continue running 2-inch lines of glue and placing the ribbon all the way around the paper until you meet the other end of the ribbon. Repeat for the other inside cover.

8 On the front cover, measure and cut a piece of the ⅛-inch-wide ribbon at the point where the cover folds. Fold the ribbon

under ½ inch for a finished look, and hot-glue in place.

9   Measure and cut 4 pieces of the ⅛-inch-wide ribbon the length of the insert frame. Hot-glue the horizontal pieces first, then overlap with the vertical pieces.

10   Put the book back together, lining up the holes. From the back of the book, run both ends of the ½-inch wide ribbon up through the two holes so the ends come out even on the top. Tie a bow.

Ribbon-Rose Ring Pillow

Alternating between the rows of ribbon roses, rows of tufted tulle
lends this dainty pillow a soft, slightly out-of-focus appearance.
Some basic sewing skills are required to create this project.

How To Make It

1 Cut two 9 x 9-inch pieces of satin. Place them right sides together and pin in place. Machine-stitch a ½-inch seam allowance around the edge leaving 6 inches open on one side. Trim the seams to ¼ inch and clip the corners. Turn right side out and push out the corners. Press.

2 Place the pillow form inside the sewn satin case through the 6-inch hole. Hand-stitch the hole closed, hiding the stitches.

3 Cut 25 six-inch-long pieces of the 2½-inch ribbon. Fold a cut piece of ribbon in half so the long edges meet. Thread the sewing needle with thread that matches the ribbon. Fold over one end of the folded ribbon from the top down, making an angle at the end. From the corner at the end, roll the ribbon, making the center of the rose. When you have rolled up about 1 inch, place two stitches at the bottom to hold in place. Keeping the thread in place, run a line of basting (large, simple stitches) down the length of the ribbon where the folded ends meet. When you get to the other end, keep the needle in place, and pull the basting line to gather the ribbon. As

Materials

¼ yard of white satin fabric

White sewing thread

Pillow form, 8 x 8 inches

5 yards of satin ribbon, 2½ inches wide

Sewing thread to match the 2½-inch satin ribbon

24 inches of satin ribbon, ½ inch wide

2¼ yards of tulle, 6 inches wide

Designer: Joan K. Morris

Tools & Supplies

Scissors

Straight pins

Sewing machine

Iron and ironing board

Ruler or measuring tape

Hand sewing needle

you are gathering, roll the rose up from the center. Once the ribbon is rolled up, stitch all the layers together at the bottom. Repeat this with the other 24 ribbon pieces.

4 Hand-stitch down the 24-inch piece of ¼-inch ribbon in the center of the pillow. Hand-stitch one of the ribbon roses on top of the center ribbon.

5 Hand-stitch in place five rows of five ribbon roses on the covered pillow. Be sure to secure

them well, by placing five or more stitches in each one.

6 Keeping the tulle in one long strand, scrunch one end together width-wise and attach it with a few small stitches to the pillow. Position it below the first rose on the top row. Move over so you are centered under and between the first and second roses of the top row. Gather about a 2-inch length of tulle in one hand, making a small loop. The loop or tuft of tulle should be loose and fluffy. Loop a piece of matching

thread several times around the base of the tulle loop to secure, and knot the thread. Cut off the ends of the thread. Hold in place using a few small stitches. Continue in this same fashion across the row, placing tufts of the tulle between the roses above it, and leaving a flowing tulle piece between each tuft. When you reach the end of a row, simply loop the tulle around the end rose as shown in the photo and continue the process on the next row.

With This Ring

Wedding rings have been part of ceremonies since at least the 12th century, and involved in the institution of marriage for longer than historians are able to pinpoint. They have even found what is believed to be wedding rings on the fingers of Egyptians buried in tombs.

During medieval times, a bride would wear a set of three rings on her hand, representing the father, the son, and the Holy Spirit. Similarly, the Elizabethans used a set of three interconnecting rings, called Gimmal rings. During engagement, the rings were separated and worn by the bride, groom, and the couple's witness, then joined together and worn by the bride after the ceremony.

It was early Romans who decided to wear a special ring on the fourth finger of the left hand. They believed that a vein in this finger, the vena amori, followed all the way to one's heart. Thus the circular ring—epitomizing eternal love—is worn on this finger.

Embossed Heart Thank You Card

This lovely thank you card provides a standout way to thank guests and attendants. To open, simply slide the tulle tie down the card. The inside is blank, to allow you to personalize each one.

Materials

Ivory premade tri-fold card with top flap (5½ x 4¼ inches when closed)

Sheet of vellum paper printed with words, 12 inches square

Sheet of solid-color embossed floral paper, 8½ x 5¼ inches

Solid-color card stock to match the embossed floral paper

Gold pigment ink

Gold embossing powder

2 gold eyelets, 3/16 inch

18 inches of tulle

Designer: Brandy Logan

New to Crafting?

Visit the appendix beginning on page 172 for an illustrated review of basic stamping, embossing, and eyelet techniques.

Tools & Supplies

Pencil

Scissors

Vellum tape or sticker machine

Glue stick

Paper trimmer

Large heart stamp

Heat embossing tool

3/16-inch eyelet hole punch and setting tool

How To Make It

1 Open the card and lay it on the vellum paper. Trace and cut the vellum to fit the outside of the card, excluding the flap. Run the cut sheet of vellum through the sticker machine or apply vellum tape (see page 175 for how to use a sticker machine). Adhere to the outside of the card.

2 Trace and cut the embossed paper to fit the flap portion of the card. Glue or run it through the sticker machine and adhere to the outside flap.

3 To make the embossed heart, press the heart stamp into the gold pigment ink and stamp the image onto the card stock. Sprinkle the image with embossing powder and heat set.

4 Carefully cut out around the outside of the heart. Set two gold eyelets in the heart's center using eyelet tools. Lace tulle through one eyelet, around the invitation, and through the second eyelet. Tie the tulle into a knot and trim the ends.

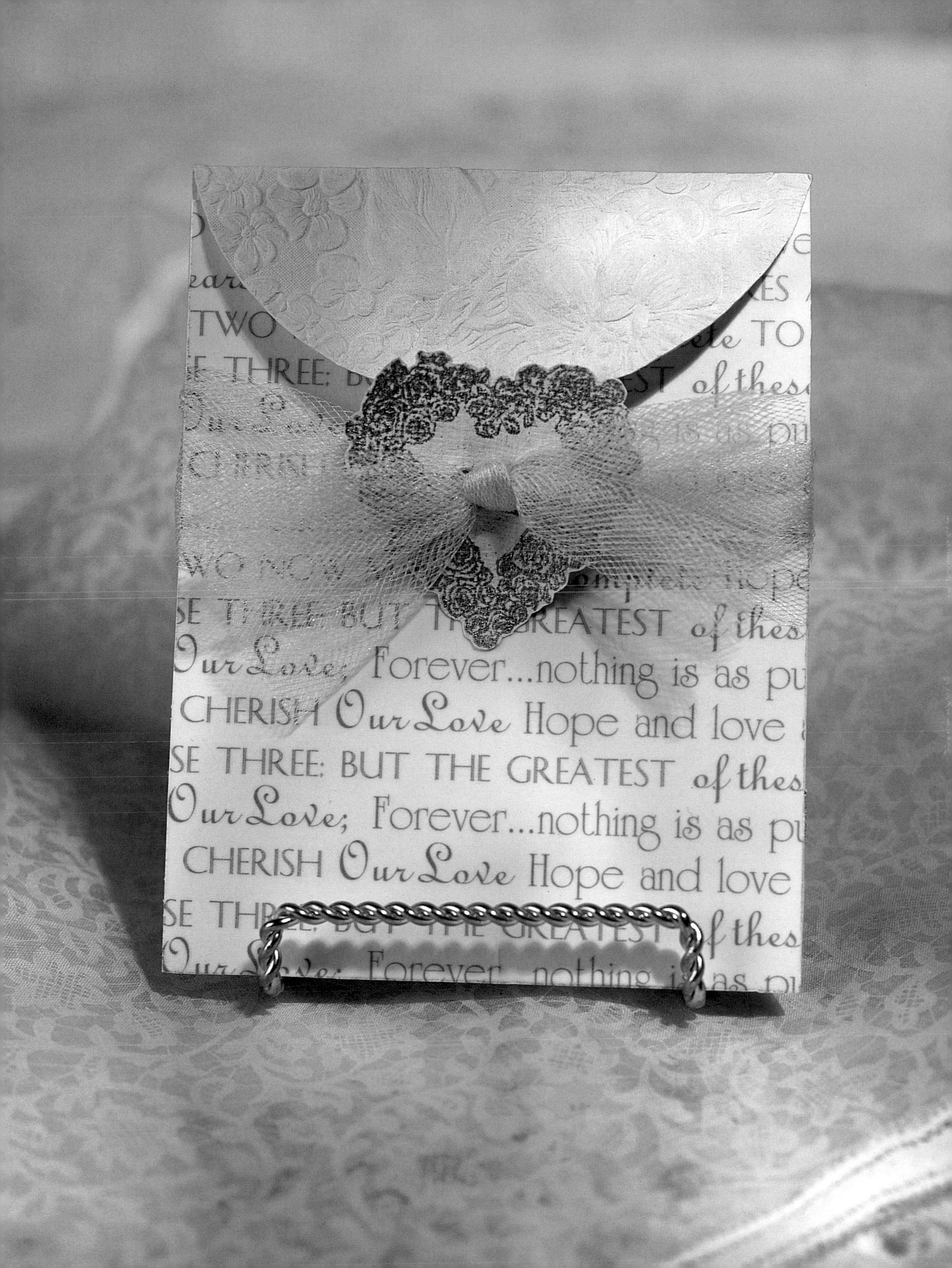

Embellished Invitations

Use a computer and printer to print out wedding information on a blank, embossed invitation. Add ribbon, charms, or adhesive-back dimensional embellishements of your choosing. If desired, mat the invitation with colored paper or card stock.

Designer: Chris Rankin

Gold-Trimmed Swan & Heart Favors

Use a gold leaf paint pen to draw decorative gold accents on a plastic swan or heart. Fill a colored favor pouch with bath salts and place in the swan; fill the heart favor with bath salts or candies, as desired.

Designer: *Linda Kopp*

Pearl & Rose Centerpiece

Cut a band of vellum long enough to fit around a glass vase. Cut a slightly narrower band out of scrapbook paper. Center and glue it to the vellum. Glue two strips of ribbon over the scrapbook paper, using the photo as a guide for position. Fill the vase with pearls and insert silk roses.

Designer: *Terry Taylor*

Our Wedding Day

Ashley

&

Grayson

Saturday, August 5, 2006

Wedding Program

Following the manufacturer's instructions, type the program wording that will appear on the inside of the program into a computer and print it out on a blank, embossed program. Cut a piece of scrapbooking paper to fit just inside the embossed outline on the cover. Print out the wording for the cover on vellum, and cut out a rectangle slightly smaller than the scrapbooking paper. Attach to the program using a sticker machine (see page 175) or glue. Glue a fabric flower to the front as shown in the photo.

Designer: Terry Taylor

Menu Card

Using decorative scissors, trim a narrow strip off the edge of the front of a ready-made card. Using regular scissors, cut a strip of scrapbooking paper slightly wider than the strip you cut off the cover. Attach the strip of colored paper to the inside edge of the card with glue or by running it through a sticker machine (see page 175). Use a computer to print the word "Menu" on a sheet of colored vellum. Cut the word out using decorative scissors and attach to the card. Thread a ribbon through the inside of the card to the outside and tie a knot.

Designer: Terry Taylor

Modern Pastels

It's your wedding, so don't be bashful—flaunt your individuality!
How about fashioning a theme around something you've always loved—
the soft hues of pastels? Our inspiration came from the delicately
diffused blues, lavenders, and pinks of the multihued hydrangea blossom.
The blooms became the focal point that ties everything together.

Hydrangeas not your flower of choice—maybe you have a
fondness for yellow roses, or a soft spot for salmon-colored lilies?
No problem! Whatever your color preference, it's a cinch to take these
inspirational ideas and transform them so they fit your own unique taste.

Modern Pastels

Celebration Bridal Bouquet

Understated but lovely, this bouquet looks garden fresh. The silk hydrangea leaves create an attractive collared effect against the green-white silk blossoms.

Materials

2 silk hydrangea blossoms with large flower bracts on long stems

9-10 snowball flowers

Florist wire

Tulle

1½ yards of double-sided wired ribbon, 2 inches wide

Tools & Supplies

Wire cutters

Scissors

Hot glue and glue gun

Designer: Linda Kopp

How To Make It

1 Pull the leaves off the hydrangea stems and set them aside for later use. They should pull off easily, leaving small plastic stubs on the stems. Remove the leaves from the snowball flowers.

2 Hold the two hydrangea stems tightly together and place the snowball flowers so the blooms completely encircle the hydrangeas. Keep the stems in place by tightly wrapping florist wire around the top of all the stems. Continue wrapping the wire down the stems for about another 3 inches.

3 Place the hydrangea leaves back on the plastic stubs of the hydrangea stems and arrange them so they form a collar around the bouquet. Secure each with a dot of glue.

4 Cut off the stems of the snowball flowers directly beneath where the wrapped florist wire ends. Beginning at the top of the stems, tightly wrap tulle around the stems and continue until you have gone about 2 inches past where the florist wire ends. Double up the tulle in the area just beneath where the florist wire ends. The tulle pads the stems and helps mask any dramatic change in the diameter of the handle.

5 Use wire cutters to trim the hydrangea stems to about 15 to 18 inches in length.

6 Find the center of the length of ribbon and place the bouquet on top of it. Position the ribbon so it is at the top of the stems. You now have two ribbon ends. Begin wrapping the stems with ribbon by bringing both ends around the stems to the front of the bouquet. Cross the ribbon pieces over each other, and then wrap the ribbon ends around to the back of the bouquet. Cross the ribbons in the back and bring them back around to the front. Repeat this process until you have wrapped approximately 10 inches of stem. Tie a bow with the remaining ribbon leaving the remainder of the stems uncovered. Cut a triangle out of the ribbon ends.

Ribbon & Bow
Favor Box Centerpiece

Everyone knows that good things come in small packages. When stacked, these miniature presents make a deliciously tempting centerpiece, and at the end of the festivities, your guests will be pleased to be able to select one to take home with them.

Materials

8-10 small paper mache boxes of varied sizes (we used round, oval, and square boxes)

Satin white spray paint

10 or more assorted color-coordinated ribbons, ranging from $1/8$ to 1 inch wide, 2 yards of each

Assorted small fabric or silk flowers

Assorted wired embellishments

Tools & Supplies

Scissors

Hot glue and glue gun

Designer: Linda Kopp

How To Make It

1 Following the manufacturer's instructions, spray paint both the inside and the outside of each box. Let dry. Apply an additional coat, if needed. Be sure to let the paint dry thoroughly between coats.

2 Line each box with decorative cupcake papers if desired, and fill with candy, soaps, or whatever you like.

3 Begin wrapping each box with ribbon using dabs of hot glue to keep the ribbon in place. Dispense hot glue sparingly making small spots and slightly pulling the ribbon over the glue so that it smears. This will help keep the hot glue from showing through the ribbon. Try to use at least 2-3 different types of ribbon on each box. Experiment with layering a gauze or net ribbon over a solid or patterned ribbon. Vary the type of bows you tie (see the project photo for ideas).

4 Embellish each box top with fabric flowers, and/or small wired pearls, crystals, and jewels. Secure with a small dab of hot glue if necessary.

Graceful Bow-Topped Cake

Like a simple dress with classic lines, this cake can easily be dressed up or down with your choice of ribbon. Choose satin and sequin-embellished ribbons as we did, or select damask, gauze, grosgrain, lace, or wired ribbon.

Materials

Two cake layers:

12-inch round cake, 4 inches

8-inch round cake, 4 inches

Buttercream icing (see recipe on page 193)

Confectioner's sugar

48 ounces of white fondant (for 12-inch layer)

24 ounces of white fondant (for 8-inch layer)

Cake board, 12-inch diameter

Cake board, 8-inch diameter

Wooden dowel, ¼-inch diameter

Royal icing (see recipe on page 96)

2 yards of satin ribbon, 2 inches wide (for bow)

1¼ yards of sequin-embellished ribbon, 1 inch wide (for bow)

Tools & Supplies

Cake leveler or serrated knife

Cake decorating turntable

Large angled spatula

Large rolling pin

Gridded roll and cut cake mat

Fondant smoothing tool

Sharp knife

Featherweight pastry bag and round tip or clean, empty squeeze bottle with a small tip

Wax paper

Scissors

Hot glue and glue gun

Designer: Juanita Mantel

How To Make It

1 Follow the cake instructions, and bake, cool, level, and ice the cake layers with buttercream icing (refer to pages 178–180).

2 Cover the cake layers with fondant (see pages 180–181).

3 Stack the cake layers (refer to pages 183–184).

4 To make the piping beads at the base of each layer, and the dots on the cake, mix a batch of Royal Icing. The consistency should pipe easily through a decorating tip, but remain firm once on the cake and not run. Use less water in the recipe for a thicker consistency. Royal Icing dries out quickly, so keep the bowl with any unused portion covered with a damp towel and plastic wrap until you're

Tip *If you are right-handed, decorate a cake from left to right, rotating the cake clock-wise as you go. If you are left-handed, simply reverse the directions.*

Royal Icing

Ingredients

3 tablespoons Meringue Powder

4 cups sifted confectioner's sugar
(approx 1 lb.)

6 tablespoons water**

Instructions

Beat all ingredients at low speed
for 7-10 minutes (10-12 minutes
at high speed for portable mixer)
until the icing forms peaks.
Makes 3 cups.

**When using a large countertop
mixer, or for stiffer icing, use
1 tablespoon less water.

ready to use it. Stir to remix the icing as needed.

5 Load the Royal Icing into a pastry bag with a round tip or into a clean, empty squeeze bottle. If you're using a plastic bottle, you can cut the tip to any size, but start small at first and make the hole larger if necessary. Hold the bag or bottle at an upright angle with the tip pointing downward, slightly above the surface. Squeeze out the icing using steady, even pressure. Keep the tip buried in the icing, but slowly raise it as the dot or bead of icing becomes larger. Once the dot has become the size you want, stop squeezing while you bring the tip to the surface. Practice piping beads and dots on a sheet of wax paper until you are satisfied with the results.

6 Pipe beads around the base of each cake tier, then pipe the dots using the project photograph as a guide for placement.

7 To make the bow topper, cut two 12-inch long pieces of the 2-inch wide ribbon. Cut a triangle out of both ends. These will be the bow streamers. Slightly cross the two ribbons in the middle and place a dab of hot glue at the intersection. Lay the 1-inch wide ribbon on top of the 2-inch wide ribbon and make a double-looped bow, hot-gluing the pieces in place as you go. Finish the bow by cutting a piece of the 2-inch wide ribbon and wrapping it around the center of the bow, making sure to cover any hot-glued areas. Attach the bow to the ribbon streamers and place on top of the cake.

8 If desired, decorate a glass cake pedestal to match the bow by hot-gluing matching ribbon to the edge of the pedestal.

Tip

When preparing to work with light-colored fondant, it is imperative to have a clean workspace, tools, and hands.

Before you begin, be sure to trim your nails and remove your rings. This will help to avoid accidental nicks and gouges in the fondant.

Floral-Sleeved Invitation

Untie the dainty ribbon and discover more bows inside this invitation, along with innovative R.S.V.P. and direction cards.

Materials

Lightly patterned scrapbook paper,
  12 x 12 inch

Striped scrapbook paper,
  12 x 12 inch

Glue stick

Solid-color scrapbook paper,
  12 x 12 inch

Floral scrapbook paper, 12 x 12 inch

2 square $^3/_{16}$-inch silver eyelets

10 inches of dot ribbon,
  $^3/_8$-inch wide

Colored polka dot paper,
  $8^1/_2$ x 11 inch

16 inches of net-and-satin ribbon
  (can also be completely solid)

24 inches of narrow satin ribbon

Repositionable glue dots

Tools & Supplies

Scissors or rotary paper trimmer

Bone folder

Glue stick

Eyelet hole punch and setter,
  $^3/_{16}$ inch

Computer and printer

Designer: Brandy Logan

Because you have shared your lives with us,
We invite you to share our joy as we exchange vows on

Saturday
May sixth, two thousand and six
6:00 pm

Greenwood Baptist Church
Atlanta, Georgia

Tracy & Timothy

Dinner and Reception to Follow

RSVP

Directions

How To Make It

1 Cut a 5 x 7-inch piece from the lightly patterned paper.

2 Cut a 7½ x 11-inch piece from the striped paper. Make sure the stripes go up and down. Bend the paper over the bone folder down the middle, and score the paper, making a crease. Run the bone folder over the crease to make a smooth edge for your card.

3 Center and attach the 5 x 7-inch patterned piece to the front side of the striped card using a glue stick or a sticker machine.

4 Cut the solid-color paper into a 7½ x 11-inch piece. Use the glue stick or sticker machine and attach it to the inside of the card. Score the card again with the bone folder.

5 Cut a 3 x 11-inch strip from the floral paper. Wrap the strip around the card to where the ends almost touch on the front of the card. Flatten the edges.

6 Remove the floral strip and set the eyelets using the hole punch and setter at each end of the strip, making sure to center them along the edges. Place the strip back over the card. Lace the polka dot ribbon through the eyelets, and tie into a bow.

7 Using a computer, print the wedding invitation wording onto the polka dot paper. Trim to 5 x 6 inches, making sure the text is centered.

8 Attach the polka dot paper with the text to the inner right-hand side of the card using the adhesive tabs.

9 Cut two 7½-inch lengths of ½-net-and-satin ribbon. Glue the ribbon on either side of the invitation paper using the adhesive tabs placed in the solid portion of the ribbon.

10 Cut a 1¼ x 7½-inch strip of the striped paper, making sure the stripes run lengthwise. Glue down the strip vertically in the center of the inner left-hand side.

11 To make the direction and R.S.V.P. cards, cut a 3 x 4-inch piece from each of the floral paper and the lightly patterned paper. Fold each in half so they measure 3 x 2 inches, and print the information inside, or use a computer to print the information and attach it inside the flap. Print "R.S.V.P." and "Directions" onto the solid-color paper, and cut the words out. Attach the words to the bottom right corners of the flaps using a glue stick.

12 Wrap approximately 10 inches of narrow satin ribbon around each card, and tie a bow. Use repositionable glue dots to attach the cards to the left side of the invitation. Refer to the project photo for placement.

13 Close the invitation, and slide the bow-tied floral paper band over the card to seal it.

New to Crafting?

Visit the appendix beginning on page 172 for an illustrated review of using a bone folder, a sticker machine, and setting an eyelet.

Many Thanks Card

Petite silver charms sewn to the front of this card accompany your note of appreciation with a pleasing jingle. Inside the card is blank, leaving you ample room to add your personal message of thanks.

Materials

Lightly patterned scrapbook paper, 12 x 12 inch

Striped scrapbook paper, 12 x 12 inch

"Thank You" charms

10 inches of narrow satin ribbon

Floral 3-D sticker

Tools & Supplies

Scissors or rotary paper trimmer

Needle and matching thread

Glue stick

Designer: Brandy Logan

The How-to & When-to of Thank-You Cards

Many people help to make a wedding memorable for a bride, and each and every one of them should be formally thanked. Phone calls, e-mails, and even preprinted cards, while time-savers, do not properly convey the personalized thanks that helpful friends, relatives, professionals, and well-wishers deserve.

Propriety dictates that handwritten notes should be sent soon after the event. Shower gifts should be acknowledged within 10 days of the party and wedding gifts within two weeks after returning from a honeymoon. Wedding gifts received before the wedding should be responded to immediately. If both a shower and a wedding gift are received from the same person, then a separate note should be sent for each gift.

In addition to sending thank-you notes to everyone who gave or sent gifts, you should also send one to anyone who provided an intangible item or service as a gift, such as the loan of a car, the use of property, homegrown flowers, or homemade food. The rule for receiving a gift from a group of people such as co-workers is this: fewer then 10, then a personal note to each; more than 10, one note placed on a bulletin board at work is considered proper etiquette. Others on your must-thank list are members of the wedding party, and the best friend who was your bridesmaid and who helped in the planning and running of your wedding—yes, even if you've already thanked her in person and have given her a gift. Wedding vendors such as photographers, caterers, and wedding consultants appreciate notes, as they help form a reference base they can use during their presentations to prospective clients.

Try to make each note warm and personal, mentioning the specific gift received and how you plan to use it. If the gift was monetary, you can let folks know they contributed to a goal you and your husband are saving for. Nice touches include referencing any special effort made on your behalf such as a special toast, or adding a wedding photo if one is available.

How To Make It

1 Cut the lightly patterned paper in half. You'll use one 6 x 12-inch strip per card.

2 Fold a strip in half to measure 6 x 6 inches. Cut the striped paper into a $2\frac{1}{4}$ x $3\frac{1}{2}$-inch strip. Make sure the stripes are running horizontally.

3 Sew the charms to the bottom of the striped strip with needle and thread.

4 Glue the striped strip as shown in the photo. Cut two 3 $\frac{1}{2}$-inch strips of narrow ribbon. Glue one on each vertical side of the striped paper.

5 Adhere the 3-D floral sticker on top of the striped paper above the charms.

Modern Pastels

Tracy & Timothy

Greenwood Baptist Church

Atlanta, Georgia

MAY 6

Save the Date

Hanging Save-the-Date Tag

This note card is so attractive, your guests will find it a welcome reminder as to when and where you are getting married. The ribbon hanger makes it easy to tack to a bulletin or message board.

Materials

Striped scrapbook paper, 12 x 12 inch

Cardboard or chipboard, 2½ x 4½ inches

Solid-color scrapbook paper, 12 x 12 inch

Black pen (optional)

12 inches of polka dot ribbon, 3/8 inch wide

12 inches of narrow satin ribbon

Flower blossom

Beaded flower

Package of adhesive-backed letters and numbers

2 white eyelets

14 inches of sheer ribbon, 3/8 inches wide

Tools & Supplies

Scissors or rotary paper trimmer

Glue stick

Computer and printer

Eyelet setter

Awl or ice pick

Designer: Brandy Logan

How To Make It

1 Cut the striped paper into a 2½ x 4½-inch strip using the rotary paper trimmer or a pair of scissors. Make sure the stripes run horizontally.

2 Use the glue stick to completely cover the 2½ x 4½-inch piece of cardboard/chipboard with the solid paper. This will be the back of your tag.

3 Cut out a 2½ x 4-inch rectangle strip from the polka dot paper. Using a computer, print the bride and groom's names to fit on the 2½ x 4-inch rectangle. Leave room to add a flower bloom as shown in the photo.

4 Center the rectangle over the striped paper, and glue in place.

5 Using the black pen or a computer, print "Save the Date" on a ½-inch strip of the solid paper, and glue it across the bottom of the tag.

6 Cut the 3/8-inch polka dot ribbon into two pieces, each six inches long. Glue one around the top and the other around the bottom of the tag as shown in the photo. Glue two 6-inch-long strips of the narrow ribbon over the seam where the 3/8-inch ribbon joins the polka dot paper rectangle.

7 Use the adhesive backed letters and numbers to place the wedding date on the 3/8-inch polka dot ribbon, as shown in the photo.

8 Glue a single bloom and a beaded flower in the center of

the card between the bride and groom's names and the date.

9 Refer to pages 174–175 and set two white eyelets at the top of the card. Thread the 3/8-inch sheer ribbon through the eyelets and tie in a bow.

What Are Save-the-Date Cards?

Save-the-date cards are the first news your guests will receive about your big event. These informal announcements are an ideal way to ensure your guests keep their calendars free and clear on your special day. They're perfect to use if your wedding is planned around a holiday or at a seasonally busy location, or if you expect a lot of out-of-town guests.

Sending save-the-date cards is a relatively new trend, so there are no set rules to go by. They may or may not match your invitation style. You could send an inexpensive postcard, refrigerator magnets, or a simple photo of the happy couple. They can even come as a brochure or booklet, with any number of embellishments or personal accents. Consider using a dramatic or spirited tone to inspire the recipient's enthusiasm.

Regardless of the style, save-the-date cards should include your names, wedding date, and ceremony/reception location. You may also wish to include accommodation and transportation information. Because this is such a new trend, many people may mistake these cards for the actual invitation, so you might want to include a note such as, "Invitation and details to follow."

Your save-the-date card should be sent at least four to six months prior to the wedding, but no later. If you're having a destination wedding, consider sending them nine to 12 months out. That way your guests will have ample time to plan their trips; they may even choose to turn it into an extended vacation. The announcements don't need to be mailed to everyone on your invitation list—just your close family and friends who you want to be sure can come.

Shades of Lavender Scrapbook Album

What more personal way to capture the memories of your wedding day than with this one-of-a-kind album? The dainty ready-made beaded flowers are a simple and pretty way to add a touch of sparkle.

Materials

Wooden album sized to hold
  12 x 12-inch pages

2 sheets of lightly patterned scrapbook paper, 12 x 12 inch

Striped scrapbook paper,
  12 x 12 inch

Floral scrapbook paper, 12 x 12 inch

28 inches of ribbon, 5/8 inch wide

32 inches of polka dot ribbon,
  3/8 inch wide

5 large silk flower blooms (we
  used hydrangea)

5 small silk flower blooms,
  in coordinating color shades

10 glass beads

8 beaded premade flowers

White rub-on word "Memories"

Solid scrapbook paper,
  12 x 12-inch sheet

Polka dot scrapbook paper,
  12 x 12-inch sheet

14 inches of narrow satin ribbon

Eight 3-D adhesive foam dots

1¼ yard of grosgrain ribbon,
  1½ inches wide

Tools & Supplies

Small screwdriver

Glue stick

Scissors

Hot glue and glue gun

Designer: Brandy Logan

How To Make It

1 Use the screwdriver and take all the hardware off the album.

2 Using the glue stick, glue a full sheet of lightly patterned paper onto the center cover of

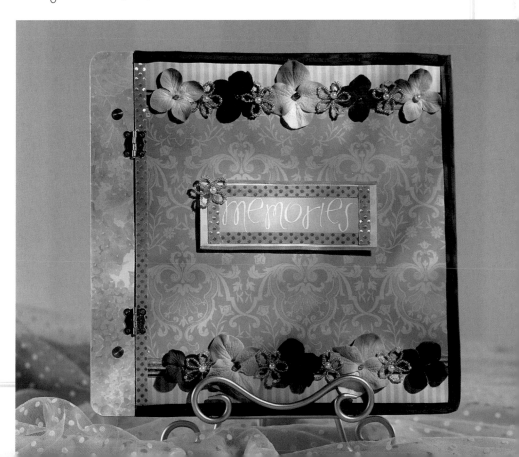

the album. Trim the edges to fit.

3 Cut two 2 x 12-inch pieces out of the striped paper, making sure the stripes run vertically. Glue one piece across the top and the other across the bottom of the cover. Trim to fit.

4 Glue the spine of the album diagonally to the back side of the floral paper. Trim any excess paper.

5 Cut the 5/8-inch ribbon in half. Use the glue stick to glue it along the edges of where the patterned paper and striped paper join. Wrap both the ends around to the reverse sides of the album cover. Hot-glue to secure.

6 Glue the 5/8-inch polka dot ribbon vertically along the left-hand side of the front cover, as shown in the photo. Wrap both the ends around to the reverse sides of the album cover. Hot-glue to secure.

7 Replace the hardware.

8 Hot-glue the silk flowers along the 5/8-inch ribbons. Alternate between large and small flowers, as shown in the photo. Glue a single glass bead in the center of each silk flower.

9 Cut the stems off the beaded flowers, and hot-glue them between the silk flowers.

10 Rub the word "Memories," or another word of your choosing, onto the solid colored paper and cut into a rectangle leaving approximately 1/2 inch around the lettering. Glue the "Memories" rectangle down on top of the polka dot paper. Trim a small border 1 inch all the way around the "Memories" rectangle.

11 Glue strips of the polka dot ribbon over the seam where the "Memories" rectangle joins the polka dot paper.

12 Add a strip of narrow satin ribbon to both horizontal edges of the polka dot paper.

13 Hot-glue a beaded flower to the upper left-hand side, as shown in the photo.

14 Attach the "Memories" board in the center of the front cover by using the 3-D foam adhesive dots. Put one in each corner of the reverse side of the board.

15 Wrap the 1 1/2-inch-wide ribbon around the top, right-hand side, and bottom edges of the album cover. Begin by placing one end of the ribbon into the crevice between the album cover and the spine, and hot-glue to secure. Slowly work your way around the edges of the album, hot-gluing the ribbon so only 1/2 inch of it shows on the front. Wrap the remaining width of the ribbon around to the back of the album cover, and glue in place.

16 If desired, purchase additional matching ribbon, and wrap the rest of the album edges.

Floral Pomander Seating Card

Adorn your reception chairs with personalized, flower-covered ornaments. Like tiny silver pearls, the center of each flower will attract your guest's attention as they search for their place with the help of this pretty take-home gift.

Materials

6 heads of blue silk hydrangea flowers (approximately 20 individual flowers are needed)

6 heads of purple silk purple hydrangea flowers (approximately 20 individual flowers are needed)

Package of 40 silver ball-headed straight pins

3-inch polystyrene foam ball

12 inches of ½-inch ribbon

Vellum paper

Floral greening pin

Tools & Supplies

Scissors

Computer and printer

Glue stick

Designer: Joan K. Morris

How To Make It

1 Pull the flowers off their stems or cut them off with wire cutters as closely as possible, leaving very little stem.

2 Place a silver ball-headed straight pin through the center of a flower from the front side. With your thumb on the pinhead, push it into the ball.

3 Alternate colors and continue placing the flowers closely together all the way around the ball until it's completely covered.

4 Cut a piece of ribbon 12 inches long. Fold the ribbon in half. Holding the raw edges of the ribbon together, push two pins through both ends. Separate the flowers, making a space to place the ends of the ribbon. Push the pins into the ball. Fold the ribbon back over the pins and place two more pins to anchor the ribbon and ensure even hanging.

5 Using a font and size that will work for a folded label measuring 1 x 3 inches, run guest names down the right side of the paper, so there is room to cut out the label. Print on vellum paper.

6 Cut out the 1 x 6-inch label with the name on the right half. Lightly fold the label in half with the name on the outside. Hold the label together and cut a triangle out of the short edge so it looks like a banner or flag. Thread the label through the ribbon with the name facing out. Place a circle of glue inside the label just to the right of the ribbon, and press the top into the glue.

Passion for Patterns Page

Decorated with soft floral, striped, and polka dot papers, this scrapbook page is light and airy, caressing your spirit like a soft spring breeze. Three-dimensional stickers come in a wide selection, so you'll be pleasantly challenged to pick just a few.

Materials

2 sheets of solid-colored paper, 12 x 12 inch

Sheet of polka dot paper, 12 x 12 inch

12 inches of net ribbon

12 inches of grosgrain ribbon

Adhesive tabs

Sheet of floral paper, 12 x 12 inch

Sheet of lightly patterned paper, 12 x 12 inch

Sheet of lavender striped paper, 12 x 12 inch

Rub-on word (we chose "Cherish")

18 inches of narrow satin ribbon

Two 3-D stickers

Sheer favor bag

Silk flower petals

Charm

Horizontal photograph

Designer: Brandy Logan

Tools & Supplies

Scissors or rotary paper trimmer

Glue stick

Sewing machine and contrasting thread (optional)

Needle

Coordinating thread

How To Make It

1 Use a 12 x 12-inch sheet of the solid paper for the background.

2 Cut a 3 x 12-inch strip from the polka dot paper and mount it near the top of the background paper, leaving an unattached area on the right side to slip two ribbons under. Slide the net and grosgrain ribbon under the polka dot paper and tie a bow in each, as shown in the photo.

3 Cut the floral paper into 6-inch-wide strips. Tear one end of one strip so the white underside shows. Mount the strip on the left side of the background page. Be sure not to extend the floral paper all the way to the left edge.

4 Cut a 7½ x 5½-inch rectangle out of the lightly patterned paper, and a 6¼ x 4¼-inch horizontal rectangle out of the solid paper. Stitch around the edge of both rectangles. Mount the smaller rectangle on top of the larger rectangle, and then mount them in the upper left-hand portion of the page, using the photo as a guide.

5 Cut a 2 x 8-inch strip of the striped paper, taking care that the stripes run up and down.

Center and rub on the word "Cherish," or a word of your choice.

6 Mount the strip on the lower right side near the bottom of the page.

7 Cut two 8-inch-long pieces of narrow satin ribbon and glue them to the top and bottom edges of the striped strip.

8 Adhere the 3-D stickers using the project photo as a guide for placement.

9 Fill a sheer favor bag with silk flower petals, and sew a charm on the bag's drawstring. Attach the bag to the lower left corner of the page.

10 Mount the focal photo.

Bridesmaid
Fragrance Gift Set

Shower your bridesmaid with presents that pamper.
The soothing scent of lavender will be a pleasant
reminder of how she helped make your wedding perfect.

Designer: Joan K. Morris

Bath Salts

Materials

Metal label holder

1 sheet of vellum, 8½ x 11 inches

Sheet of floral scrapbooking paper

Bead-stringing wire

Assorted silver and colored glass beads

White bath salts

Soap dye (we used lavender)

Lavender head sachet

Cork-topped bottle, 3½ x 5 inches

Tools & Supplies

Computer and printer

Scissors

Glue stick

White craft glue

Wire cutters

Small glass or ceramic bowl

How To Make It

1 Pick a font on your computer for your bridesmaid's name. Do a trial run on scrap printer paper to make sure it will fit in the label holder. Print the name on the vellum.

2 Cut out both the name and a piece of floral paper the same size so they fit in the label holder. Use the glue stick to attach the vellum to the floral paper.

3 Paint a thin line of white craft glue around the inside edge of the label holder, and place the paper facedown onto the glue.

4 Use the wire cutters to cut a 15-inch length of the beading wire. Insert one end through one of the label holder's holes, and tie two square knots, leaving a ½-inch tail. Start placing the beads onto the wire, alternating colors, sizes, and shapes. Bead until you have just enough wire to tie two more square knots, again leaving a ½-inch tail. Run the tails back through the beads at both ends until the wire is hidden.

5 To color the bath salts, place enough salts to fill the bottle in the small bowl. Add the soap dye, a few drops at a time, and mix until you get the desired color. Mix in a couple tablespoons of the lavender heads.

6 Place the bath salts in the bottle, and replace the cork. Hang the beaded name holder around the bottle.

Designer: Joan K. Morris

Soap

Materials

Easy-melt clear glycerin soap

Soap fragrance

2 soap molds

Lavender head sachet

2 sheets of 12-inch-square scrapbooking paper (1 sheet each of
defferent patterns)

6 inches of ribbon, ⅛ inch wide

6 inches of ribbon, ½ inch wide

Tools & Supplies

Microwave-proof glass container

Microwave

Metal spoon

Measuring spoons

Clear plastic wrap

Ruler

Scissors

Hot glue and glue gun

How To Make It

1 To make two bars of soap, follow the manufacturer's instructions to melt the clear glycerin
soap in the glass container. It
will take ten 1-inch cubes to
make a bar measuring about 3 x
4 inches. Use the metal spoon
to stir. Once the soap is melted,
add a couple drops of fragrance, and stir.

2 Pour the melted soap into
each mold until it is one-third
full. Sprinkle 1 teaspoon of the
lavender head sachet per bar
over the top of the melted
soap. Let harden 10 minutes.
Repeat the layers two more

times. Let harden for 1 hour
before pushing the soap out of
the molds.

3 To prevent the soap from
staining the wrapping paper,
wrap the bar in clear plastic
wrap. Cut out two pieces of
patterned paper to wrap around
each bar like a present, using
hot glue to hold the paper ends
in place.

4 Cut out two more pieces
of paper in a different pattern. Each piece will be 4
inches wide and long enough
to wrap around the width of
the bar. Fold both edges over
1 inch lengthwise so the
width now measures 2 inches.
Wrap the paper around the
middle of the bar, and attach
with hot glue.

5 On one bar, wrap a piece
of the ½-inch mesh ribbon
down the center of the folded
piece of paper, and attach the
ends with hot glue. Place a
piece of the ⅛-inch ribbon
down the middle of the mesh
ribbon, and hot-glue the ends.
For the second bar, attach
only the ½-inch plaid ribbon
in the same way.

Designer: Joan K. Morris

Decoupage Box

Materials

Round paper mache box with lid, 6x3 inches

3 sheets of 12-inch-square scrap-booking paper (1 sheet each of three different floral patterns)

36 inches of ribbon, ½ inch wide

Tools & Supplies

Scissors

1-inch paint brush

Decoupage glue

Ruler or tape measure

Hot glue and glue gun

How To Make It

1 Cover the paper mache box in the three different patterns of scrapbooking paper. First decide which pattern you want to use for the interior, for the outside of the lid, and for the outside of the box.

2 Cut out the pieces of paper you'll need. Attach the paper by using the paintbrush to apply a thin coat of the decoupage glue to the box and lid. It's best to attach the paper 3 inches at a time. Use your fingertips to gently smooth away air bubbles, working from the middle outward.

3 Apply an even coat of the decoupage glue to the entire box and lid, inside and out, to protect the paper and give it a shiny finish. Let dry.

4 Cut two pieces of the ½-inch mesh ribbon so that each piece is long enough to stretch from the inside edge of the lid, across the top, and then back under to the inside edge on the opposite side. Attach the ends of the first ribbon to the inside edges of the lid with dabs of hot glue. Repeat with the second ribbon, crisscrossing it at right angles with the first.

5 Using 24 inches of the ½-inch mesh ribbon, hot-glue three loops on top of each other to form a bow, and clip the ends at an angle. Position the bow where the two ribbons cross each other on the top, and hot-glue in place.

Lavender Sachet

Materials

Mesh favor bag, 4x6 inches

Lavender head sachet

24 inches of ribbon, ½ inch wide

Tools & Supplies

Scissors

Ruler or tape measure

How To Make It

1 Fill up the mesh favor bag with the remaining lavender heads, pull the drawstrings closed, and knot.

2 Cut 24 inches of the ½-inch mesh ribbon, and tie in a bow around the top of the bag.

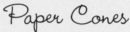

Paper Cones

Cut a square out of scrapbook paper, form it into a cone, and glue the seam closed. Wrap ribbon around the cone, and glue in place. Cut two pieces of ribbon for streamers, and attach them to the front of the cone. Following the manufacturer's directions, drip sealing wax over the ribbon, and press with a seal (see photo for placement).

Designer: Linda Kopp

CD Case Favor

Type and print out the bridal couple's name and wedding date on a piece of scrapbooking paper. Trace a circle that is slightly smaller than the CD tin around the type, and cut it out.

Attach the circle to the tin, using a sticker machine (see page 175), or with glue.

Tie a tulle bow and attach fabric flowers and pearl wedding embellishments.

Designer: Linda Kopp

Simple Seating Cards

Using a computer, print guest names on one side of a sheet of blank place cards and a table number on the other side.

Cut two small slits, centered in the top front of the card. The slits should measure the width of your ribbon. Thread the ribbon through the slits, from the front of the card to the back, then back up to the front.

Hot-glue small fabric flowers and pearl embellishments under the center portion of the ribbon.

Designer: Linda Kopp

Embellished Favor Tin

Hot-glue a ribbon around the base of a tin. Center a sticker on the tin's lid.

Designer: Linda Kopp

Fanciful & Fun

It's the happiest day of your life—you're getting married! So go all out, have fun, and bring a smile to everyone else's face, too. Use a touch of the fanciful to set a bright, joyful, and wonderfully witty mood. The lighthearted tone is just right for capturing that "walking on air" feeling that surrounds the day. Show off your kicky attitude, your confident sense of style, and your one-of-a-kind view of the world. You're the type of gal who marches to the beat of her own drummer, the woman who kicks off her shoes and dances barefoot, the one with a sunshiny, carefree perspective.

Fanciful Daisy Cake

Is there any combination that expresses sheer joy and exuberance more than daisies paired with polka dots? The alternating round and square cake layers add to the whimsical appearance.

Materials

Three cake layers:

12-inch round cake, 4 inches tall

10-inch square cake, 4 inches tall

8-inch round cake, 4 inches tall

Buttercream icing (see recipe on page 193)

48 ounces of white fondant (for 12-inch layer)

24 ounces of white fondant (for 8-inch layer)

10 ounces of white fondant (for polka dots)

½-ounce jar of yellow icing color

Confectioner's sugar

36 ounces of white fondant (for 10-inch layer)

Adhesive-backed roll of shiny paper, 20 inches wide

Cake board, 12-inch diameter

Roll of tulle, 6 inches wide

Wooden dowel, ¼-inch diameter

Cake board, 10-inch square

Cake board, 8-inch diameter

Round fondant cutout, 1½-inch diameter

26 silk daisy heads

Tools & Supplies

Cake leveler or serrated knife

Cake decorating turntable

Large angled spatula

Large rolling pin

Gridded roll and cut cake mat

Fondant smoothing tool

Pencil

Scissors

Measuring tape

Clear cellophane tape

Poly blade or pizza roller knife

Small rolling pin (we used a 9-inch pin)

Extruder or piping bag

Scissors

Ruler

Pencil

Designer: *Joan K. Morris*

How To Make It

Covering the Layers with Fondant

1 Follow the cake instructions, and bake, cool, level, and ice the cake layers with buttercream icing (refer to pages 178–180. In order to cover the bottom and the top layers of cake with yellow fondant, you need to mix all the yellow at once—forty-eight ounces for the bottom layer, 24 ounces for the top layer, plus about 10 ounces for the dots on the center layer. If you can't work with that much fondant at one time, cut the amount in half and try to add the same amount of the yellow icing color to each half. Then mix the two halves together.

2 Cover the bottom and the top layers with yellow fondant (see pages 180–181). To keep fondant from sticking to the rolling pin or mat, lightly dust the surfaces with confectioner's sugar. Place the remaining yellow in a plastic bag so it won't

dry out. Let the remaining yellow fondant sit for a couple of hours before you cut out the circles.

3 Cover the square middle layer with white fondant. (refer to page 182).

Decorating the Cake Board

4 Roll out adhesive-backed paper with the adhesive side up. Place the 12-inch cake board on the adhesive side of the paper, leaving at least an inch of paper all the way around. Draw around the circle. Remove the cake board. Cut out a circle one inch larger than the circle you drew. Remove the protective paper backing to reveal the adhesive. Place the cake circle in the center of the adhesive. Cut slits in the paper about every inch or so around the cake board. Fold the edge of the paper over to the back of the cake board, and smooth it down.

5 Measure around the cake board circle. Double the measurement and cut a piece of tulle in that length. Fold the tulle in half lengthwise, so it's 3 inches wide. You don't need to fold the whole length at once, just

fold as you go. Place one end of the folded tulle so the open sides line up with the outside edge of the cake board. Tape in place. Work your way around the cake board, folding 2-inch pleats in the tulle as you go. Tape each pleat in place on the inside of the circle so the cake hides the tape. Do this all the way around the cake board.

Making & Attaching the Fondant Decorations

6 Stack the cake layers (refer to pages 183–184).

7 Let the fondant sit on the layers for an hour. Using the round cutout and starting on the top layer, cut circles out of the fondant. Lightly press the cutter into the fondant, turn it, and pull it out. The circle of fondant should come out with it. If it doesn't, just remove it with a knife. Remove circles all the way around the top layer.

8 Using the smaller rolling pin, roll out some white fondant. Cut out the same number of circles that you removed from the top layer. Place the white circles where the yellow circles were removed. Roll over the circles on the cake layer

until the edges join. Don't press too hard.

9 Repeat this on the bottom layer. For the middle layer, roll out the yellow fondant to place into the cutout circles.

10 Use an extruder or piping bag to pipe a line of fondant along the base of each cake layer. Pipe yellow fondant for the base of the bottom tier, and white fondant for the second and third tiers.

11 Cut the daisy heads off their stems, leaving about a ¾ inch stem. Place the daisies onto the cake by pushing them into the fondant. remember to remove the daisies before serving the cake.

Polka-Dotted Toasting Flutes

Here's to love, happiness, and just plain fun. Add to the gaiety of any proclamation with these toast-worthy flutes. Make a bride and groom set, or provide one for each guest to have and to hold, and to take home.

Materials

Champagne flutes, 9 inches tall

Round easy-peel stickers,
 ³/4-inch diameter

Frosted glass spray (make sure it
 is food-safe)

2 yards of colored wire, 22-gauge

Assorted colored, glass beads

Tools & Supplies

Masking tape

Scrap paper

Craft knife

Measuring tape

Wire cutters

Designer: *Joan K. Morris*

How To Make It

1 Clean the flutes. Place masking tape around the inside rim of the flute, and the area at the top of the stem to protect them from the spray. Wrap a piece of paper covering the whole stem, and tape in place. Wrap a piece of paper inside the flute, and tape in place.

2 Evenly space the round stickers all the way around the cup portion of the flute. Be sure and rub the stickers down to prevent the spray from getting underneath them.

3 Spray the flutes with food-safe frosted glass spray, following the manufacturer's instructions. Apply the spray in light, even coats. The more coats you apply, the more opaque the glass will become. Let dry.

4 Remove the tape, the paper, and the stickers. They should peel off easily. If they don't, use a craft knife to peel up the edges and pull them off. If there is an area with over-spray, lightly scrape it off with a craft knife.

5 Cut a 36-inch-long piece of wire for each flute. Start placing the beads onto the wire, alternating the size, shape, and color, until you have 10 inches of beads. Center the beads on the wire.

6 Hold both ends of the beading so the beads don't slip off, and start wrapping the bead string around the stem of the flute. When you have all the beads wrapped around the stem, wrap the end of the wire around the bottom of the stem a few times and then back up under the beads to hide it. Do the same thing with the wire end at the top.

I'd Like to Propose a Toast

Today virtually all areas of the world have a celebratory drinking toast, which is declared before imbibing. The act of raising one's glass and toasting may have originated as early as 12th-century Europe, where drinkers placed spiced toast in a cup of wine or ale to add flavor and absorb the sediment. As this tradition waned, revelers commenced drinking to a specific woman's name, presumably in hopes that the female's name would "spice" the drink's flavor in place of the bread.

According to one fable, the first wedding toast began in France, where scorched bread was placed at the bottom of the newlyweds' wine glasses, challenging the duo to a race. The spouse who drank the wine and ate the bread first would be the ruler of the couple's household.

Another tale says Rowena, the daughter of a Saxon leader, made the very first toast at a feast in Saxony. As legend has it, Rowena toasted the British king, saying, "Lord King, be of health." King Vortigern, being overwhelmed by her gesture, married her that very night.

Whatever the derivation, toasting a bride and groom has become a conventional blessing, filled with sentimental discourse or good-natured jesting.

Traditionally, the best man is expected to toast the pair with a short speech or poem. Allowing more of the wedding party to give individual toasts is growing in popularity, which sometimes includes the parents toasting the couple and the two toasting each other.

Brad
All the Best
Lots of Love,
Love to you both! Rosemary
Happily Ever After
You're the perfect couple! Darcy
Best Wishes! Love, Shannon
Congratulations you two!
Here's to a Great Future!
What a lovely wedding

Sweetheart Signature Frame

Invite your friends to write their good wishes and sage words of advice on the mat surrounding a picture of you and your sweetie. Make sure to have them sign before you place the mat into the frame.

Materials

Wood frame

Craft paint

Border stencil

Modeling paste

Matte spray sealer

Colored card stock, 12 x 12 inches

Photo mat board, 5 x 7 inches

Photograph

2 sheets of patterned scrapbook paper

Tools & Supplies

Paintbrush

Ruler

Spray adhesive (repositionable)

Spoon

Palette knife

Masking tape

Scissors

Pencil

Craft glue

Glue stick

Decorative-edged scissors

Cellophane tape

Designer: *Joan K. Morris*

How To Make It

1 Remove the cardboard from the inside of the frame and save for later. Paint the entire frame including the front, side edges, and the inside edges. Let dry.

2 Place the center of the stencil design in the center of one side of the frame. Spray the back of the stencil with spray adhesive and replace it in position. Following the manufacturer's instructions, place a teaspoon-size dab of modeling paste on the stencil. Use the palette knife to push the modeling paste into the stencil. Don't push too much; make sure you leave some height to the design. Carefully pull off the stencil from one end. If you make a mistake, just wipe the modeling paste off and start over. Repeat this procedure on the other three sides. Let dry.

3 Repeat this process in each corner. If your stencil doesn't have a corner design, find the center of the design and tape over one-half of the stencil. Place the uncovered half of the stencil in the corner and apply the modeling paste. Let dry. Take the tape off the stencil, and tape the other half. Place it running the other direction from the corner and apply the modeling paste.

4 Once all of the modeling paste has dried, apply a second coat of craft paint. Let dry. Spray the frame with matte spray sealer.

5 Using the glue stick, glue the 12 x 12-inch card stock to the cardboard that you saved from the frame. Place it back in the frame.

6 Cover a 5 x 7-inch mat with scrapbook paper and insert a photo. Using decorative-edged scissors, cut a rectangle 1/2 inch larger than the photo mat. Glue the rectangle to the photo mat, center in the frame on the card stock, and tape or glue in place.

Beaded Napkin Ring

Here's a project that does double duty: a festive napkin ring and then it's a brightly colored bracelet that will remind your guests of all the fun they had at your wedding.

How To Make It

Materials

Bracelet-size memory wire

Assorted colored glass beads

Jump rings, ¼ inch

Tools & Supplies

Measuring tape

Wire cutters

Needle-nose pliers

Designer: *Joan K. Morris*

1 Use the wire cutters to cut one 22-inch-long piece of bracelet-size wire for each napkin ring. To keep the beads from slipping off, bend about ½ inch of one end into a small circle with the pliers.

2 At the other end, start stringing beads. Continue until you are about 1 inch from the straight end. Don't go any farther, or the beads will start slipping off. Remember to alternate beads of different sizes, colors, and shapes.

3 Use the pliers to bend the wire's straight end into a small circle. Open one of the jump rings by using the pliers to twist the ends away from each; twisting instead of pulling helps retain the ring's circular shape. After placing a small bead onto the jump ring, insert it onto the wire circle and twist closed. Repeat on the other end. Your beaded ring is ready to place around a napkin.

Daisy Flower Girl Basket

A tisket, a tasket, a sweet flower girl basket.
Silk daisies top a flounce of tulle on this pretty basket.
Fill with rose petals—or daisy heads.

Materials

Wooden or wicker basket
with handle

White spray paint

Tulle circles

8 silk daisies

Assorted ribbon, (three coordinating colors, various widths)

Tools & Supplies

Scissors

Hot glue and glue gun

Designer: *Linda Kopp*

How To Make It

1 Spray paint the basket white, both inside and out. Let dry. Apply a second coat if necessary.

2 Remove the silk leaves from the daisy stems. Pull the daisy heads off their flower stems. Closely cut off any remaining stem from the flower.

3 Hot-glue a piece of ribbon around the rim of the basket. Center a narrower length of ribbon over the first, and glue in place.

4 Fold a tulle circle in half. Pinch the middle of the folded side, and make gathers in the tulle. Center the pinched area near the top of the rim on a side without a handle, and hot-glue in position. Repeat on the opposite side of the basket.

5 Hot-glue a large daisy over the pinched tulle area, and a smaller daisy on either side, as shown in the photo. Repeat on the other side of the basket.

6 Hot-glue a line of daisy leaves across the handle, and a daisy at the base of each handle where it connects to the basket.

7 Knot a length of ribbon around the base of one handle, behind the daisy, leaving two long streamers. Tie a shoelace bow in the same place, leaving streamers.

Fanciful & Fun

Lemon Candy Gel Candles

Shining like little rays of sunshine, festive lemon hard candies can be glimpsed through etched polka dots. Poured into its own glass container, the pink gel candle is a pleasing contrast against the candy.

Materials

Gel candle wax

Red wax color

4-inch bleached wick with metal tab

Round double-wall glass candle holder, 3 ½ x 5 ¼ inches

Round stickers, ¼ inch in diameter

Frosted glass spray

Masking tape

Hard lemon candy

Tools & Supplies

Clip-on candy thermometer

Candle-making pouring pot with spout

Disposable metal spoon

Craft knife

Designer: *Joan K. Morris*

How To Make It

1 Following the manufacturer's instructions, clip the candy thermometer onto the pouring pot, and then melt the gel candle wax in it. When the wax has reached the recommended temperature, use the disposable metal spoon to stir in the red wax color, a little at a time, until you're satisfied with the color. Remember: You can always add more color. Removing it is impossible.

2 Place the 4-inch wick in the candle holder's insert, and carefully pour the melted gel wax into the insert to the desired height, a little at a time. Check the wick periodically and adjust its position, if necessary. Let cool for a few hours.

3 After the candle has thoroughly cooled, remove the insert from the bowl, and set aside. Place the ¼-inch round stickers evenly all around the outside of the bowl. (The low-tack stickers used to price items at yard sales work well.) Make sure you've pressed them down firmly so the frosted glass spray doesn't seep under the edges.

4 Cover the top of the bowl with strips of masking tape, leaving the entire outside surface of the bowl uncovered. Following the manufacturer's instructions, apply the frosted glass spray to the outside of the glass bowl. It should take two or three coats, depending on how opaque you want the bowl to be. Let dry.

5 Remove the masking tape and the stickers. If there is any underspray, scrape it off carefully with the craft knife.

6 Place the lemon candy inside the bowl, and reinsert the candle.

Beaded Bridesmaid's Bracelet

Fond memories will surely pop into your bridesmaid's head each time she reaches for this pretty bracelet. Use colors from your wedding, or personalize it by fashioning it in her favorite color.

Materials

Stretch bead cord, .7mm diameter

Swarovski crystal metal sliders

Silver beads, 4mm diameter

Tools & Supplies

Measuring tape

Scissors

Instant glue (optional)

Designer: *Linda Kopp*

How To Make It

1 Loosely measure around the recipient's wrist and note the measurement.

2 Begin stringing beads on the cord, starting with a slider. Thread the cord through one of the slides on the back of the slider, then through three metal silver beads. Repeat the pattern until you have strung enough beads to match the wrist measurement.

3 Cut the cord off the spool, allowing yourself another six inches of empty cord. Bring both ends of the cord together, and tie with a single overhand knot. Pull the knot tight and make a second overhand knot. For added security, place a drop of instant glue between the two knots, and then pull tight.

4 Repeat Steps 2 and 3, except thread the cord through the other slide.

The Perfect Bridesmaid Dress

No two people share the exact shape, so to make all of your bridesmaids feel equally beautiful, consider choosing an A-line dress silhouette—a style that is flattering to all shapes and sizes. Or, if you'd prefer not to have a cookie-cutter wedding party, choose the color and fabric for the gowns, and let your bridesmaids choose their own dress style. Most importantly, although it's your day, you want everyone to look and feel his and her best.

Tiny Bubble Wands

*Transform adults into big kids with the wave of a wand—
a bubble wand, that is. Bubbles never seem to lose their magic,
so what better way to end a magical day than with a bubbly send-off?*

Materials
Roll of tulle, 6 inches wide

26-gauge colored wire

Assorted small beads

Package of bubble wands

Tools & Supplies
Ruler

Scissors

Wire cutters

Needle-nose pliers

Designer: *Joan K. Morris*

How To Make It

1 Cut a piece of tulle 6 inches long. Fold it in half twice making four layers, each a 3 x 3-inch square. Cut each square shape into a circle. To speed this step up, you can cut through all four layers of tulle at once.

2 Cut three pieces of wire, two 4-inch-long pieces, and one 7-inch-long piece.

3 Line up the ends of the three pieces of wire. Push all three ends through the center of all four layers of tulle until 1 ½ inches of wire has been pushed through. Fold the tulle up to the 1½-inch side of the wires, and pinch the center. To achieve the "flower" look, wrap the other end of the long piece of wire three or four times around the pinched part of the tulle. Keep wrapping the wire down the other two wires to their ends.

4 Place a colored bead on the short end of each wire, and use the needle-nose pliers to wrap the wire around the bead to hold it in place.

5 Run the long end of the wrapped wire through the hole at the top of the bubble wand. Bring the end up and twist it around the wire to hold it in place. Place the bubble wand loosely in a holder for easy access.

Stamped Thank You Card

Using decorative scissors, trim a narrow strip off the edge of the front of a ready-made card. Using regular scissors, cut a strip of scrapbooking paper slightly wider than the strip you cut off the cover. Attach the strip of colored paper to the inside edge of the card with glue or by running it through a sticker machine (see page 175). Using the photo as a guide, stamp a flower image and the words "Thank You". Glue a small fabric flower as shown.

Designer: Terry Taylor

Favor Tins

Center and glue a pressed flower to the lid. Use hot glue to attach a narrow ribbon around the base portion of the tin.

Designer: Joan K. Morris

Daisy-Embossed Invitation

Use colored chalk to color over the embossed daisy design. Color the center of the flowers with a highlighter, then dab that area with a tissue. Lightly spray the card with a chalk fixative, following the manufacturer's instructions. Type the invitation wording onto a sheet of vellum and print out. Trim the vellum to fit under the daisies and within the embossed area, as seen in the photo. Use a double-slitted press paper punch to punch through the top corners of the vellum and the invitation. Thread a ribbon through the slits, and tie a knot. Punch a series of double-slits along the bottom portion of the card, using the photo as a guide for the spacing. Weave a ribbon through the slits.

Designer: Joan K. Morris

Ring of Daisies Place Card

Use hot glue to attach fabric flowers around the oval opening of a fabric photo frame. Hand-write or use a computer and printer to print guests' names out on scrapbook paper or card stock. Trim to fit, and insert into the frame.

Designer: Terry Taylor

Quick & Easy

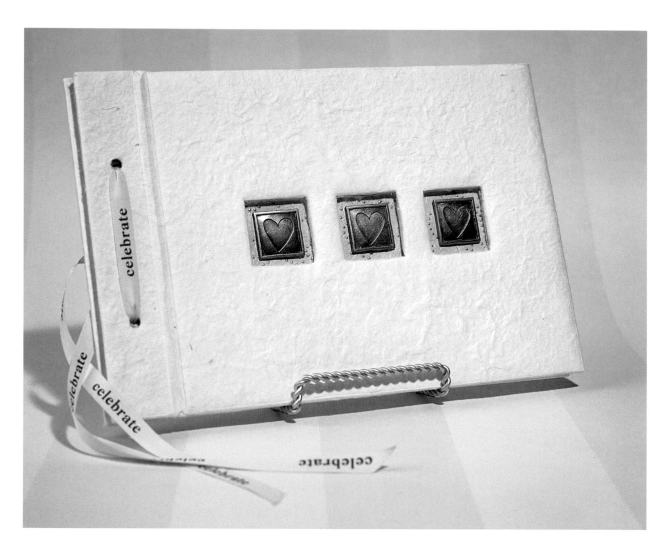

Charm Guest Book

Purchase a guest book with inset squares on the cover. Remove any decorations attached inside the squares. Cut squares of scrapbook or specialty paper and glue them in the inset areas. Center and attach an adhesive-backed metal charm to each square. Replace the ribbon binding with ribbon of your choice.

Designer: Linda Kopp

Beaded Cake Server Set

String beads of varying size, color, and shape onto colored wire. Be sure to leave plenty of space between the beads. Wrap the wire and beads around the handle, beginning at the bottom and working your way to the top.

Designer: Joan K. Morris

Mini Glass Favor

Cut a slit to the middle of a piece of round tulle. Turn the plastic glass upside down and hot-glue the slit-area of the tulle to the base where the stem meets the glass. Fill the glass with candy-coated almonds. Gather the tulle up over the almonds, and tie with a ribbon. Add a small silk flower.

Designer: Linda Kopp

Bold & Bright

She's daring and trendsetting and oh-so-thoroughly modern. This describes the bride who creates new traditions for others to follow rather than follow what others have done before. That's why she pores through the latest fashion magazines and stays on top of what's in style and ahead of the crowds. Her taste tends toward the bold and minimal, toward geometrics and bright-hot colors that dazzle. She goes for the unexpected, the sure-to-surprise—and you can be certain that whatever she chooses for her wedding will make a powerful, original statement about who she is.

Square Stacked Cake

Angular and sleek describe this minimalist cake. Brightly colored flowers with matching ribbon project a crisp, modern look.

How To Make It

1 Follow the cake instructions, and bake. Cool, level, and ice the cake layers with buttercream icing (see pages 178–180).

2 Cover the cake layers with fondant (see pages 180-182). To keep the fondant from sticking to the rolling pin or mat, lightly dust the surfaces with confectioner's sugar..

3 Stack the layers in position using cake boards and dowels (see pages 183-184).

4 Measure around each cake layer, and cut the ribbon to those measurements plus one inch.

5 Wrap the lower edge of each layer with the corresponding ribbon length. Hold the

Materials

Three cake layers:

12-inch square cake layer, 4 inches tall

10-inch square cake layer, 4 inches tall

8-inch square cake layer, 4 inches tall

Buttercream icing (see recipe on page 193)

Confectioner's sugar

72 ounces of white fondant (for 12-inch layer)

48 ounces of white fondant (for 10-inch layer)

36 ounces of white fondant (for 8-inch layer)

Wooden dowel, ¼-inch diameter

Cake board, 12 inches square

Cake board, 10 inches square

Cake board, 8 inches square

4 yards of colored ribbon, 1½ inches wide

Flat-head pins, ½ inch long

4 large bright colored silk flowers

Tools & Supplies

Cake leveler or serrated knife

Cake decorating turntable

Large angled spatula

Gridded roll and cut cake mat

Large rolling pin

Fondant smoothing tool

Measuring tape

Scissors

Designer: Joan K. Morris

ribbon in position by placing two of the ½-inch pins at one end of the ribbon. *Important:* Be sure all the pins are removed before serving the cake. Fold the extra length of ribbon under, and pin in position using two pins, one at the top and one at the bottom of the ribbon.

6 Cut the stems of the flowers three inches long. Stick them into the center of the top cake layer as shown in the photograph.

Flower Power

Be they silk or fresh, flowers are becoming an increasingly popular choice for use in cake decorating. Whether cascading down layers, or simply sprinkled atop the cake, flowers are both an affordable and attractive addition to any cake. When using real flowers, make certain that the blooms are pesticide-free, and that you're not serving up poisonous or toxic flowers. Popular edible varieties include: calendula, pansy, marigold, lavender, violet, and nasturtium. If desired, you can add a bit of glamour by first crystallizing edible flowers (such as pansies and violets) by coating them in egg white and superfine sugar. Other nontoxic flowers to consider include orchids, tulips, gardenias, daisies, and roses. If you're using flowers from your garden, wash them and let them dry on a paper towel, then place them in plastic bags and freeze until you're ready to use them.

Bright Bride's Bouquet

This fashion-forward bouquet has slender leaves orbiting a round form of bold flowers. Echoing the flower colors is a reversible ribbon tied in a simple bow.

Bold & Bright

Materials

Brightly colored silk flowers in two
contrasting colors

Narrow bright and dark green
silk leaves

2 yards of reversible ribbon,
½ inch wide

Tools & Supplies

Scissors

Hot glue and glue gun

Wire cutters

Designer: Joan K. Morris

How To Make It

1 Begin with one center flower
(we chose a hot pink one), and
then place a circle of contrast-
ing-color flowers around the
first flower. For our project this
meant five orange flowers surrounding the hot pink one.
Continue adding circles of flowers in alternating colors. We
used a circle of eight hot pink
flowers followed by a circle of
four orange flowers. As you add
flowers, bend the heads out or
down so the bouquet takes on
an overall round shape.

2 Hot-glue loops of narrow
leaves to the bouquet in a ran-
dom pattern. Our leaves were
about 7 to 8 inches long; if
yours are longer, cut them
before creating the loops.

3 Cut the stems to a seven-
inch length. Hold them
together tightly, using a rubber
band to help hold them tem-
porarily if necessary.

4 Cut a length of ribbon and
center the stems in the middle
of it, just below the base of the
flowers. Bring both ends around
to the front, cross the ends over
each other, and take them
around to the back of the bouquet. Repeat this process until
the stem is wrapped in ribbon.
Secure the ribbon in the back
of the bouquet with hot glue.

5 Tie a length of ribbon
around the top of the stems,
leaving the ends long to serve as
streamers. Using another length
of ribbon, tie a simple bow so
that the reverse color shows.

Tip: For our size flowers, nine
of each color were needed.
The number of flowers
you need will vary
depending on their size.

Bride's Side or Groom's Side

*"Are you with the bride or the
groom?" is the question courteously
asked at weddings, and the answer
leads to a conversation rather than a
deadly brawl. Though this tradition
is something we take for granted
today, separate seating for the bride
and groom's families during the nup-
tials originally had more to do with
keeping the peace than keeping any
kind of tradition. In ancient times,
marriages were often arranged for
political reasons. Brides were sometimes given as offerings to create
peace between warring tribes, so
seating the families on separate sides
avoided bloodshed at the wedding.*

*The custom of the bride standing on
the left side of the groom is also a
vestige of more violent times.
Kidnapping brides was once a common practice. Often, the groom
would hold onto the bride with his
left hand so that he could use his
right for dueling with other suitors.*

Box-Fold Invitation

Like a flower opening to the sun, this card gracefully unfolds to reveal the wedding invitation. Despite its impressive design, this card is quite easy to make—but your amazed friends and family won't know that.

Materials

Purchased premade blank card with folding flaps (or template, page 196)

Cream-colored card stock (one sheet if using a purchased card, two if using the template)

Textured and patterned papers (enough to cover each flap, inside and out)

Yard of ribbon, 3/8 inch wide

Metal ribbon charm

Tools & Supplies

Scissors

Bone folder

Glue stick or craft glue

Computer and printer

How To Make It

1 Use a premade, purchased card or photocopy the template on page 196 and cut the shape from the card stock. Place the template over the card stock shape, and use the bone folder to fold where indicated.

2 Glue textured or patterned paper onto the inside of each of the card's flaps, both inside and outside, and then trim with the scissors.

3 Use the computer and printer to print your invitation information onto a sheet of card stock. Cut the card stock to fit into the center of the invitation, and glue it down.

4 Close the invitation by overlapping the flaps just as you close the flaps of a cardboard box.

5 Wrap the ribbon around the closed invitation. Thread each end through the metal charm, and then tie a knot. Trim the ribbon's ends by cutting at an angle.

Mr. and Mrs. Richard Johnson
invite you to share in the ceremony
uniting their daughter

Linda Elaine

to

Chris Anthony Kopp

on Sunday, the twenty-seventh of
August
two thousand and six
at one o'clock in the afternoon

St. Philip Presbyterian
Bedford, Texas

Designer: Brandy Logan

Bright Geometrics Centerpiece

Sleek aluminum mesh, mirror diamonds, and row upon neat row of brightly contrasting flowers make for a striking centerpiece. Shorten or lengthen the arrangement to suit the size of your reception table by adding or subtracting boxes of flowers.

Materials

3 square boxes,
 each 7 x 7 x 3 inches

Roll of wrapping paper

24 mirrors, 1-inch square

32 mirrors, ½-inch square

16 x 32-inch silver mesh screen

3 squares of polystyrene,
 7 x 7 x 2-inch

Package of Spanish moss

Greening floral pins

24 brightly colored flowers

24 contrasting brightly colored
 flowers

Tools & Supplies

Scissors

Glue stick

Hot glue and glue gun

Measuring tape

Keyhole saw or serrated knife (to
 cut polystyrene)

Wire cutters

Designer: Joan K. Morris

How To Make It

1 Cover the outside of the boxes neatly with wrapping paper. Use a glue stick to adhere the paper and carefully rub out any bubbles. Use hot glue to attach the sides of the boxes together in a line.

2 Hot-glue the mirrors diagonally onto the sides of the boxes in the pattern shown in the photograph.

3 Place the boxes in the center of the 16 x 32-inch mesh. Fold the mesh up along the long edges. Cut to the corner of the mesh with scissors. Fold the mesh up and over the top. Fold the short edges up, cut off the extra at the sides, and then fold the sides up and over. Push the corner edges together.

4 Cut the polystyrene to fit and set them inside the boxes.

Place a layer of Spanish moss over the foam and hold it in place with five greening floral pins in each box.

5 Cut the stems of the flowers to 3 inches in length. Place two rows of one color of flower down the center of the boxes, eight flowers per box. Try to keep the flowers at the same level all the way across, and place a dab of hot glue on the bottom of the stems as you go.

6 Place a row of the other color flowers on both sides of the center flowers, again keeping the flowers at the same level.

Tip *The number of flowers needed may vary, depending on the size of your flowers.*

Menu

Appetizer
Grilled Crabcake with Remoulade
On a Bed of Grilled Vegetables &
Mesclun Greens

Salad
Romaine with Goat Cheese, Sliced
Cherry Tomatoes & Fresh Chervil
With Lemon Thyme Vinaigrette

Entrée
Filet Mignon au Poivre with Brandy
Peppercorn Sauce
Medley of Baby Vegetables
Saffron & Cabernet Whipped Potatoes

Dessert
Chocolate Royal & Praline Crunch

Wedding Cake

Textured-Paper Menu

What's for dinner? To find out, guests may check their menu, presented on textured paper and held neatly in place with colorful brads.

Materials

4 colored brads, 1/8 inch

3 sheets of textured specialty paper

Tools & Supplies

Scissors

18-inch ruler

Decorative scissors

Computer and printer

Hole punch, 1/8 inch

Designer: Joan K. Morris

New to Crafting?

Visit the appendix section on pages 173–174 for a review on how to use decorative scissors and brads.

How To Make It

1 Use decorative scissors to cut out a 4 x 5-inch piece of paper. Use regular scissors to cut out a 5 x 7-inch and a 3 x 5-inch piece.

2 Select a font and type the menu text into a computer. Print it out on the 3 x 5-inch paper.

3 Center the papers on top of one another in order of descending size. Punch a hole through all three layers of paper at each of the smallest paper's corners. Insert a colored brad in each hole.

Nuts (Jordan Almonds) to You

At many weddings, Jordan almonds are often given as guest favors. The historic basis for the offering of these candy-coated nuts originates from the Middle East where each guest receives five pieces of the candy to correspond to the five wedding wishes: happiness, longevity, fertility, health, and wealth. The candy coating symbolizes the sweetness of marriage, while the almond represents the bitterness.

Pyramidal Candy Boxes

This little pyramidal container makes a big visual impact!
For the most eye appeal, choose three colors of paper
and mix and match different textures.

Materials

Template (page 196)

Scrap paper

Assorted solid and patterned
 brightly colored papers

1/8-inch eyelets in colors that
 match paper

1/3 yard of ribbon, 1/8 inch wide

Candy of your choice

Tools & Supplies

Pencil

Ruler

Scissors

Decorative scissors

Glue stick

1/8-inch hole punch

Eyelet tool

Tack hammer

New to Crafting?

Visit the appendix section on pages
173–175 for a review of using deco-
rative scissors and setting an eyelet.

How To Make It

1 Enlarge and trace the two triangle templates found on page 196 on scrap paper. Cut both out.

2 Use the larger template to cut a 7-inch triangle out of a sheet of solid-colored paper. Set the template aside, and place the newly cut triangle, right side down, on a flat surface.

3 Measure and draw a line 1/4 inch in from the edges on all three sides of the triangle. Cut off the top 1/4 inch of each of the paper triangle's points. Fold in the sides on the lines you've just drawn.

4 Leaving the triangle's sides folded in, place the 3-inch triangle template in its center, positioned so each of its three points intersects the center of one the triangle's three folded sides. Lightly trace the template. Remove the template and fold in on the lines

to create a pyramid (you'll need to trim the folded points so the pyramid closes completely).

5 Use the 3-inch triangle template and the decorative scissors to cut triangles from three of the assorted decorative papers. Adhere the triangles to the sides of the pyramid using the glue stick.

6 Use the 1/8-inch hole punch to make a hole 1/4 inch down from each of the pyramid's points. Place an eyelet into the hole in the paper's front, and use the eyelet tool and the tack hammer to secure the eyelet. Use a different color eyelet at each point.

7 Fill the pyramid with candy.

8 Thread the ribbon through the eyelets at all three corners and tie a bow at the top.

Designer: Joan K. Morris

Save-the-Date
Bottle Cap Magnets

When struck with a hammer, a simple, ordinary bottle cap magically
transforms into a contemporary, miniature decorative frame.
Add a bit of wedding information, tuck into a sleek pillow envelope,
and you have a knock-your-socks-off announcement.

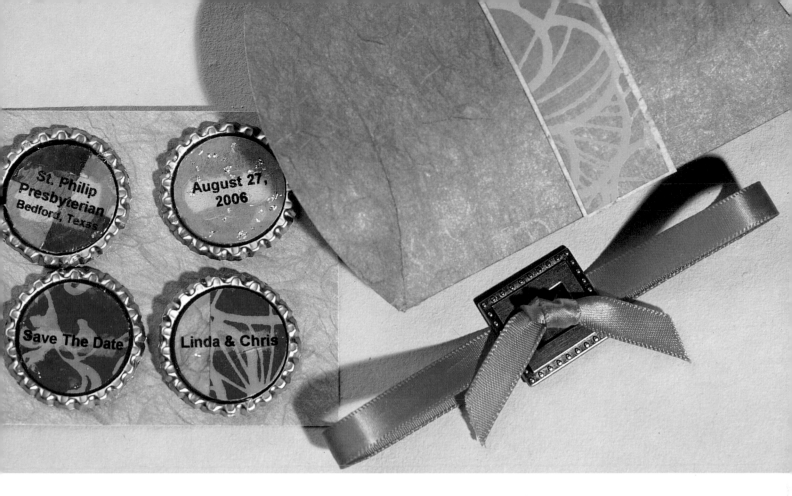

Materials

4 unused bottle caps

Small scraps of 5 different
  patterned papers

1 printer-ready transparency sheet

Craft glue

Clear embossing ink

Clear embossing powder

4 small round magnets

2 sheets of solid-colored textured
  paper (in contrasting colors)

Temporary adhesive

Envelope template (page 195)

½ yard of ribbon, ⅜ inch wide

Metal ribbon charm

Designer: Brandy Logan

Tools & Supplies

Rubber mallet or hammer

Old magazine

Old book

1-inch circle press punch

Scissors

Glue stick

Computer and printer

Heat embossing tool

Hot glue and glue gun

Photocopier (optional)

How To Make It

1 Place one bottle cap top side
down on an old magazine rest-
ing on a hard surface. Place a
book on top of the bottle cap,
and pound with the rubber mallet or hammer until the sides of
the cap roll under. Repeat for
the other three bottle caps.

2 Use the circle punch to
punch out a circle from a different patterned paper for the center of each bottle cap (see
page 174 for more information
on punching paper). You can
also layer wedges or partial
circles from different papers to
create unique designs—use the
glue stick to attach the various
layers.

3 Use a computer and printer to print the following onto the transparency sheet: Save the Date, your names, the location, and the date. Cut each of these items from the transparency, and glue each one down onto a paper circle.

4 Press the face of each paper circle onto the clear embossing ink, and then sprinkle it with the clear embossing powder. Set with the heat embossing tool, referring to the basic instructions on page 173 if needed. Repeat this procedure to add another layer to each paper circle.

5 Hot-glue each circle onto a bottle cap, and then hot-glue a magnet onto the back of each cap.

6 Cut a 3½ x 3-inch rectangle out of one sheet of solid-colored paper. Use temporary adhesive to attach the bottle caps to the paper. Set aside.

7 Trace or photocopy the envelope template on page 195, and cut out. Set the template on top of the other sheet of solid-colored paper and cut out the shape. Leave the pattern on top and use the tip of a pair of closed scissors to score the fold lines (open scissors may tear the paper).

8 Remove the template and fold the paper shape on the horizontal fold lines, and then hot-glue the flap to the inside. Cut a 3¼ x 1-inch strip of solid-colored paper that contrasts with the envelope's color, and hot-glue it vertically to the center of the envelope front. Cut a 3⅛ x ⅞-inch strip from a patterned paper, and hot-glue it on top of the solid-colored strip.

9 Place the paper with the bottle caps attached inside the envelope, and fold the side flaps in.

10 Wrap the ribbon around the envelope, thread each end through the metal charm, and tie in a knot. Trim the ribbon ends by cutting at an angle.

Wedding Announcements

While traditionally the bride's parents announce the wedding of their daughter, today it is quite common for the bride and groom to announce the event. Send the announcement to anyone not invited to the ceremony or reception that you'd like to tell about the marriage, your married name, and your new address. Take care to not make them feel left out. In essence, you are letting them know you are sorry they couldn't be with you that day and that you care about them.

Wedding announcements are just that—announcements. They are not an invitation, and the giving of gifts is purely optional. They are sent after the wedding has taken place, and can even be postmarked and sent on the wedding day, but never before. Any time up to one year after the event is considered acceptable.

Framed Seating Card Display

Streamline reception seating with this colorful seating card display. Increase the frame size or the number of frames to accommodate the number of guests on your list. Using printer-ready place cards makes quick work of even the most extensive guest list.

Materials

Metal frame with backing material (ours is 18 x 22 inches)

Roll of wrapping paper

3½ yards of satin ribbon, ¼-inch wide (your amount may vary based on your frame size)

Printer-ready place cards

Solid-colored textured paper

Patterned textured paper

Scrap of patterned contrasting textured paper

Tools & Supplies

Scissors

Tape

Straightedge or ruler

Pencil

Computer and printer

Paper trimmer

Glue stick

Border punch

Designer: Brandy Logan

How To Make It

1 Remove the backing from the frame and cover it with the wrapping paper. Attach the paper by taping it to the back of the backing material.

2 Use the straightedge or ruler and the pencil to draw straight, evenly spaced horizontal lines across the wrapping paper. The number of lines needed will depend on the size of your frame and your number of seating cards. Our 18 x 22 frame has seven lines for a total of 21 seating cards.

3 Cut strands of ribbon about 3 inches longer than the lines. Using the pencil marks as guides, tape one end of each ribbon to the back of the backing material, stretch it tight across the front, and tape the other end to the back on the other side. When all the ribbons are taped on, place this assembly back into the frame.

4 Use the computer and printer to print guest names along the bottom edge of the printer-ready place cards.

5 Use the paper trimmer to cut a ¾-inch-wide strip off the top flap of each place card, so the printed name shows when the flap is folded down.

6 Use the paper trimmer to cut a piece of solid-colored textured paper the same size as the front flap. Glue this paper onto the flap.

7 Use the paper trimmer to cut a piece of patterned textured paper the same size as the front flap. Use a border punch to cut a decorative border on one long edge of the paper, and then glue this paper on top of the solid-colored paper (the solid color should show through the decorative border). See page 174 for more about using paper punches.

8 From the scrap of contrasting paper, use the paper trimmer to cut a ⅛-inch-wide strip the length of the place card. Use the paper trimmer again to cut a small rectangle from the patterned paper that matches the front flap (make sure it fits inside the place card above the printed names). Attach the strip above the printed names on the inside of the place card, and then add the rectangle to the center of the strip.

9 Use the computer and printer to print the word "Table" with a table number below it (one each for as many as you need) onto a sheet of solid-colored paper that matches the solid paper used on the front flap. Use the paper trimmer to cut one of these table numbers into a rectangle just slightly smaller than the rectangle created in the previous step. Glue this on top of the first rectangle.

10 Alphabetize and slip each card over a ribbon.

Mini Purse Thank You Card

These jaunty little purses aren't intended to hold your lipstick, but rather a note of thanks. Bright and clever, they're sure to impress. For added fun, add a small picture or two from the wedding.

Materials

Sheet of patterned paper

Sheet of white card stock

Scrap of patterned paper in contrasting color

Small square brad

8 inches of ribbon in coordinating color, 3/8 inch wide

Temporary adhesive

Tools & Supplies

Template (page 195)

Photocopier (optional)

Scissors

Bone folder

Hot glue and glue gun

Designer: Brandy Logan

New to Crafting?

Visit the appendix on pages 174 and 176 for an illustrated review of how to use brads and a bone folder.

How To Make It

1 Trace or photocopy the template on page 195 and cut out. Lay the patterned paper, right side down, on a flat surface and place the template, right side up, on top of it. Cut the template shape out of the patterned paper.

2 Keep the template on top of the patterned paper, and use the bone folder to score the fold lines. Remove the template, and fold the patterned paper shape to create a "purse" that can sit upright.

3 Cut a 2 x 9-inch strip from the card stock. Fold the card stock strip accordion style into four 2¼ x 2-inch rectangles. Write your message of thanks on the card stock, and then hot-glue one end of the strip to the front of the inside fold on the bottom of the purse.

4 Cut the scrap of contrasting patterned paper into a 1⅛ x ¾-inch strip. Insert the brad into the center of one end of this strip. Hot-glue the other end of the strip to the flap at the top of the purse.

5 Hot-glue the ends of the 8-inch length of ribbon together to form a loop. Place the ribbon loop inside the purse to create a handle (make sure the glued ends are hidden inside the purse).

6 Attach temporary adhesive to the inside of the little strip to keep the purse closed.

bride

groom

Cherish

Husband

Wife

June 18th, 2005

Wedding Scrapbook Page

Sleek metal words and bold, die-cut flower images momentarily interrupt the linear lines of this scrapbook page. The clever use of adhesive foam dots gives the photograph its eye-catching three-dimensional look.

How To Make It

Materials

1 sheet each of lime green, orange, and hot pink polka-dot paper, 12 x 12 inches

Sheet of white card stock, 12 x 12 inches

Adhesive tabs

24 inches of polka-dot ribbon, 3/8 inch wide

1 strip each of cream-colored and silver paper, 11 x 1/8 inches

Vertical photo

Sheet of white paper

Metal photo corners

Adhesive foam squares

Die-cut flower images

Metal words

Sheet of light green card stock

Tools & Supplies

Scissors or paper trimmer

Ruler or straightedge

Liquid paper glue

Computer and printer

Oval paper punch

Designer: Pamela Frye Hauer

1 Mount the lime green polka-dot paper onto the card stock. Using the photo as a guide to size, cut one strip from the orange polka-dot paper and a narrower strip from the hot pink polka-dot paper, saving the scraps for later use. Layer these vertically on either side of the lime green polka-dot paper.

2 Cut the ribbon into two 12-inch strands, and use the liquid paper glue to attach them to the green polka-dot paper, referring to the project photo for placement. Add the cream-colored and silver paper strips to the orange and pink polka-dot sections.

3 Enlarge your photograph if desired. Cut the white paper into a rectangle that's about 1/8 inch larger than your photograph on all sides. Then use the orange and hot pink polka-dot paper scraps saved in step 1 to make a rectangle that's about 1/4 inch larger than your photograph on all sides. Use these to double mat your photograph.

4 Attach metal photo corners to the matted photograph, add adhesive foam squares to the back, and mount it in the center of the green polka-dot section.

5 Cut the die-cut flower images in half and attach them as shown in the project photo. Attach metal words running down the left side of the page.

6 Print the wedding date onto the light green card stock and punch it out using an oval paper punch (see page 174 for more about using a paper punch). Attach the oval below the photo.

Mini Champagne Flute Tosses

Wrap a reversible ribbon around a glass and tie a pretty knot. Trim the ribbon ends at an angle. Slip the ribbon off the glass. Fill the glass with heart-shaped rice and cover with a piece of round tulle. Slip the knotted ribbon back over the tulle and glass.

Designer: Linda Kopp

Brad & Ribbon Place Card

Following manufacturer's instructions, type a guest name into a computer, and print it out on a sheet of perforated place cards. Using a hole punch, make a small hole in each corner of the front of the card. Insert a colored brad into each hole. Wrap a narrow ribbon around the brads.

Designer: Linda Kopp

Unity Candle

Wrap a length of ribbon around the center of a pillar candle and hot-glue the ends to secure in place. Center, wrap, and glue a narrower, gauze ribbon over top. Repeat the steps above and attach additional bands of ribbon, using the photo as a guide for placement. Hot-glue a metal charm over the center ribbon.

Designer: Terry Taylor

Favor Tin

Cut a circle of colored vellum the same size as the clear plastic on the tin lid.
Use a press punch to punch a circle or square out of scrapbook paper and
stamp an initial in the middle. Glue the initial square in the middle of the vellum
circle. Punch holes around the edge of the vellum, using various shaped hole
punches, and then glue to the inside of the lid.

Designer: Joan K. Morris

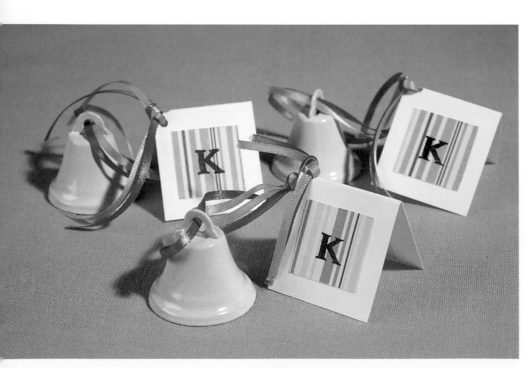

Well-Wishes Bell

Cut a square out of a place card.
Use a press punch to punch a
square out of patterned scrapbook
paper. Stamp an initial in the middle
of the patterned paper. Let dry, then
glue to the place card square. Punch
a small hole in the corner of the
place card. Thread narrow ribbon
through the bell loop, then through
the card, and then tie a knot.

Designer: Linda Kopp

Paper-Wrapped Guest Book

Cut a wide strip of patterned scrapbook paper. Make sure the strip is long enough to wrap vertically around the cover of your ready-made guest book. Type the words "Guest Book" into a computer, and print it out on a sheet of vellum. Trim the vellum to fit the width of the scrapbook paper, and run it through a sticker machine (see page 175). Attach the vellum to the paper. Punch two holes and insert brads, using the photo as reference for placement. Run ribbons through the spine of the guest book, and tie.

Designer: Linda Kopp

Basic Craft Techniques

One of the wonderful things about the crafting industry is that it doesn't stand still. The selection of tools and materials is constantly improving and expanding—offering new options to make creating easier, and allowing crafters to be even more creative. Whether this is your first venture into crafting (welcome!), or you are an accomplished crafter, refer to this section to introduce or refresh yourself on some key basic techniques and tools used throughout this book.

stamping

Stamping can transform just about any type of paper from plain to extraordinary. The basic techniques are simple to master.

1 Secure the paper you'll be stamping in place with masking tape.

2 Just lightly tap the stamp on the surface of the ink pad; don't press the stamp into the pad or rub it across the pad's top.

3 Test the inked stamp on scrap paper. If the image is too faint, re-ink the stamp; if the stamp is over-inked, blot it on a paper towel.

4 Holding the stamp firmly, press down on the paper without rocking or moving the stamp. Press each corner of the stamp carefully.

5 Lift the stamp straight up without rocking or moving it. Clean the stamp as directed by the manufacturer between colors or after each stamping session.

embossing

Once the trademark of a specialty printing process, embossing still retains its cache, yet is easy for the home crafter to master.

1 To emboss an image, begin by following Steps 1–5 on the facing page, using embossing ink instead of stamping ink.

2 Immediately after stamping, while the ink is still wet, cover the stamped image with a layer of embossing powder.

3 Shake the excess powder off the stamped image and onto a piece of scrap paper so you can return it to its original container for later use.

4 Turn on your embossing gun and hold it over the embossed surface to activate (melt!) the embossing powder, referring to the manufacturer's instructions. Allow the embossed areas to harden before handling.

cutting paper

Decorative-edged scissors have created a world of creative opportunity for crafters. For good results, use long, smooth motions to cut your paper. For perfect corners and pattern matches, you may need to make several practice cuts to get just the look you want.

Cleaning Stamps

To clean a stamp, simply press it onto a paper towel moistened with water and commercial stamp cleaner. Non-alcohol baby wipes can be used instead, and the moisturizers in them will help condition the rubber.
Some inks will stain your stamps. Don't worry—these stains will not affect the color of future stampings as long as you clean your stamps well between use.

punching paper

Craft manufacturers have come a long way since the days of the simple hole punch, and today's punches are fun and easy to use.

1 To use a press punch, insert the paper in the punch, carefully aligning the punch pattern on your paper. Press down gently but firmly — voila!

2 To use a squeeze punch, insert the paper in the punch, aligning the punch pattern as directed above, and squeeze.

3 To punch thin papers such as tissue paper, you may need to add bulk to get clean edges on your punched shapes. To add bulk, simply place a sheet of medium-weight paper behind the tissue paper. Layering multiple sheets of tissue paper often works as well, depending on the sharpness of your punch.

using brads

To use a brad, make a small hole on the right side of your paper with a paper piercing tool or embroidery needle. Press the closed brad into the hole, open the wings on the back side of the paper, and press to secure in place.

setting eyelets

Eyelets are beautiful embellishments and can be functional, too, as they can be used to affix other decorative elements to your hand-crafted cards.

1 Place the paper you'll be adding the eyelet to on a piece of cardboard or an old magazine. Use a pencil to lightly mark the paper where you want to add the eyelet.

2 Use the punch end of the eyelet setting tool to make a hole at the pencil mark by hitting the top of the tool with a small hammer.

3 Push the eyelet through the hole so that its front side is on the front side of the paper. (If you want to use the eyelet to attach something to the paper, push it through that item first.)

4 Turn the paper over so the front of the eyelet is facing down. To anchor the back of the eyelet in place, first match the eyelet setting tip to the size of your eyelet.

5 Position the tool over the eyelet, and hit the back of the setting tool with a small hammer.

making stickers

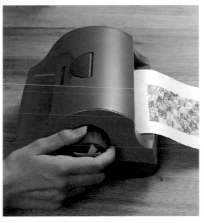

1 Trim your paper to no greater than the maximum width the machine allows.

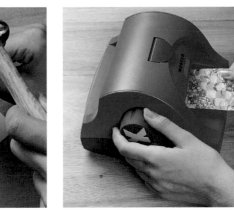

2 Insert the paper into the machine and twist the handle until the paper comes out the opposite side.

3 Use your adhesive-backed paper as is, or, if you're feeling really adventurous, cut out fun sticker shapes with a die-cut machine or a paper punch.

using a bone folder

To use a bone folder, simply move it down a folded crease or other paper surface you'd like to smooth, pressing firmly but gently.

making a blank card

Although blank cards are readily available, you have complete creative control when you make your own, because you can design every detail, choosing the type of paper and the size.

1 After you've decided on the size of your card, cut a piece of card stock that measures twice that size. For example, to make a 4- x 5-inch (10 x 12.5 cm) card, cut a piece of card stock that is 8 x 5 inches (20 x 12.5 cm). If you plan to insert your card in a premade envelope, your card should be approximately ⅛ to ⅜ inch (3 to 9 mm) smaller than the envelope so it slides in easily.

2 On the inside of the card stock, lightly mark the midpoint. Place a metal ruler along this midpoint and use a bone folder to score along this line from one end to the other. Scoring breaks the top layer of the paper fibers and makes it easier to create a crisp fold.

3 Fold the card in half along the scored line. To sharpen the fold, press slowly yet firmly along the fold with the curved edge of the bone folder.

NOTE: To add a decorative border to your card, cut the front edge with a pair of decorative-edged scissors or tear it against a deckle-edged ruler.

Will Your Card Survive the Mail?

Absolutely, as long as you take the necessary steps to protect your special, one-of-a-kind creation. Because handmade cards are often made with bulky or heavy materials and may be in an envelope that is an unconventional size, you should take the extra effort to protect your card. An extra layer of paper wrapped around the card before placing in an envelope can make all the difference. It's wise to take your cards to the post office so each item can be properly weighed and stamped as "fragile." Your card—call it mail art if you want—may require additional postage.

cutting windows

So simple to make, a window allows you to create special effects and add exciting imagery such as photographs and photocopies.

1 Measure and mark the area for the window on the front side of your card.

2 Cut out the window with a sharp craft knife, switching to a new blade if your cuts aren't clean and smooth.

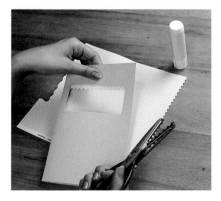

3 If desired, layer a border (or multiple borders) on the inside of the card to show through the window.

making multilayered cards

Multilayered cards are a great way to showcase specialty papers such as vellums. Choose papers that are distinctly different in color and texture for best effect.

1 To make a multilayered card, first make multiple blank cards with the same dimensions. Pierce holes about an inch (2.5 cm) from the edges of the fold line at top and bottom.

2 Align the cards so their right sides face up, then thread an embroidery needle with 12 inches (30 cm) of ribbon, yarn, colored wire, or embroidery floss. Insert the threaded needle through the hole at the top edge of the card on the inside and bring it up on the outside of the card. Unthread the needle, then return to the inside of the card. Rethread the needle and bring it up through the hole closest to the bottom edge and out on the front side.

3 Turn the card over and tie the ribbon in a bow along the spine of the card. Trim off any excess.

Working with Fondant

Preparing the Cake

The designs in this book start with a cake covered in fondant—so let's begin with one of the most important fondant fundamentals—getting the cake ready for the fondant.

Level & Fill Cakes

Start by baking a cake using firm-textured batter, such as pound cake or fruitcake. Let cake cool at least one hour, then level off the crown.

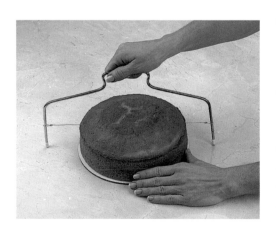

1 Leveling. Using a cake leveler: Place cake on a cake circle. Position ends of the cutting wire into notches at desired height.

With legs standing on work surface, cut into crusted edge using an easy sawing motion, then gently glide through cake

Using a serrated knife: Place cake on a cake circle and then onto a cake decorating turntable. While slowly rotating the turntable, move knife back and forth in a sawing motion to remove the crown. Make sure to keep the knife level as you cut.

2 Filling. The filling, usually buttercream icing, helps hold cake layers together and adds flavor. Fill a decorating bag with buttercream without placing a tip on the coupler or use tip 12. Make a dam by squeezing out a circle of icing ¼ inch from the outside edge of the cake. This will help prevent filling from seeping out. Fill inside the circle with icing, using a small angled spatula to spread (preserves or pudding may also be used).

3 Place next layer on top, making sure it is level.

Ice Cakes

Before covering with fondant, cakes must be lightly iced to seal in moisture and to help fondant stick to the cake. There are two easy ways to ice.

USING THE CAKE ICER TIP

1 This is the fastest way to get a smooth surface. Trim a 16 inch decorating bag to fit tip 789. Fill bag half full. Starting in center of cake top, hold bag at a 45° angle, lightly pressing the serrated edge of tip against cake. Squeeze a ribbon of icing in a continuous spiral motion to cover cake top, with last ribbon forcing icing over the edge of cake top.

2 To ice the sides, squeeze icing as you turn the cake slowly on the cake turntable. Repeat the process until the entire cake side is covered.

3 Smooth the sides of the cake by leveling the icing with the edge of the large angled spatula. For easier smoothing, it may help to dip the spatula into hot water, wipe dry and glide it across the entire surface.

Smooth the top using the end of the spatula. Sweep the edge of the spatula from the rim of the cake to its center. Then lift it off and remove excess icing. Rotate the cake slightly and repeat the procedure, starting from a new point on the rim until you have smoothed the entire top surface.

USING A SPATULA

1 Gliding your spatula on the icing is the trick to keeping crumbs out of the icing. Never allow your spatula to touch the cake surface. Place a large amount of icing on the center of the cake top. Spread across the top, pushing toward the edges.

2 Cover sides with icing. Create smooth sides by holding the spatula upright with its edge against the side. Slowly spin the turntable without lifting the spatula from the icing surface. Return excess icing to the bowl and repeat until sides are smooth.

3 Smooth the sides and top with the spatula, following step 3 for "Using the Cake Icer Tip".

Tip

Practice covering a cake in fondant at least two weeks prior to the wedding.

Covering Round Cakes

How do you cover a cake with fondant that's perfectly smooth, without wrinkles or air bubbles? The flexibility of fondant is your secret weapon. Just follow the instructions for the right ways to knead, roll out and lift the fondant, and you'll find that covering a cake is easy.

1 Prepare cake by covering with buttercream icing.

2 Before rolling out fondant, knead it until it is a workable consistency. If fondant is sticky, knead in a little confectioner's sugar. Lightly dust your smooth work surface and your rolling pin with confectioner's sugar to prevent sticking. Roll out fondant sized to your cake. To keep fondant from sticking, lift and move as you roll. Add more confectioner's sugar if needed.

3 Gently lift fondant over rolling pin and position on cake.

4 Shape fondant to sides of cake with a fondant smoother. We recommend using the smoother because the pressure of your hands may leave impressions on the fondant.

Use the straight edge of the smoother to mark fondant at the base of cake. Trim off excess fondant using a spatula or sharp knife.

5 Smooth and shape fondant on cake using the smoother. Beginning in the middle of the cake top, move the smoother outward and down the sides to smooth and shape fondant to the cake and remove air bubbles. If an air bubble appears, insert a pin on an angle, release air and smooth the area again.

Covering Large Round Cakes

Cakes 14 inches and larger require extra care in covering. Don't use a rolling pin to lift the larger amount of fondant needed. Instead, use the safer cake board method described here.

1 Cover cake with buttercream icing. Roll out fondant sized to your cake.

2 Slide a large cake circle that has been dusted with confectioner's sugar under the rolled fondant. Lift the circle and the fondant and position over your cake. Gently shake the circle to slide the fondant off the board and into position on the cake.

3 Smooth and trim as described in the "Covering Round Cakes" instructions.

Calculating the Size

Here's the easy formula for figuring the size you need to roll fondant to cover a round, square or sheet cake. Measure top of cake across center and add height of each side. Roll out fondant to that size, ¼ inch thick.

For example, 8 inch 2-layer cake: 8 inch top + two 4 inch sides = 16 inches diameter fondant. For petals, ovals, hearts and hexagons, you would use the same formula—just remember to measure at the widest area of the top of the cake to determine the size.

Covering Square Cakes

Don't let the sharp corners of a square cake intimidate you. It's easy to use your hands to shape fondant around the corners, so you finish with perfectly smooth edges.

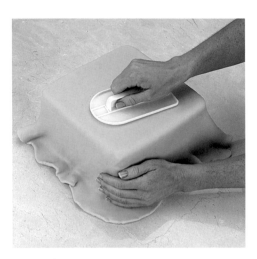

1 Position fondant on cake, smoothing the top with the fondant smoother. Pull the corner flaps gently out and away from the cake; smooth the corners with hand to eliminate the creases. Smooth sides with the smoother.

2 Trim off excess fondant at bottom with a spatula or sharp knife.

3 To give a finished look, smooth top, all sides and bottom edge of cake again with the smoother.

Covering Base Boards

Give your cake a dramatic look by placing it on a base board covered with fondant. Cut cake boards 2 inches larger in diameter than your cake, unless otherwise directed, then roll out fondant about 1 inch larger than board size. Wrap board with foil.

1 Lightly coat board with piping gel to help the fondant stick to the foil.

2 Roll out fondant to desired size, ¼ inches thick. Position over board using a rolling pin, draping fondant over edge.

3 Trim excess fondant from edges under bottom of board. Smooth top and sides with a smoother.

How many dowel rods do you need?

The larger the cake you're supporting, the more dowel rods you'll need. If the top cake is 10 inches or less, use six ¼ inch wooden dowel rods or four white plastic dowel rods. For 16 and 18 inch cakes, use eight dowel rods—we recommend the wider plastic dowel rods for these larger cakes because they provide more support.

Stacked Construction

In this most popular method of cake construction, cakes are placed directly on top of one another to create a great architectural look. The cakes must be supported and stabilized by dowel rods and cake boards, cut to size. After you've covered each cake with fondant, it's time to prepare them for stacked construction.

1 Mark the bottom cake for placement of dowel rods. This is done using the cake above it for size reference. Center a cake board the same size as the cake above it on the base cake. Using a toothpick, trace the board edge; dowel rods will be placed within this traced outline.

2 Insert one dowel rod into cake, straight down to the cake board. Make a knife scratch on the dowel rod to mark the exact height. Pull out dowel rod.

3 Cut the suggested number of dowel rods (see note at left) the exact same height, using the marked dowel rod as a guide.

4 Insert dowel rods into cake, spacing evenly 1½ inches in from the imprinted outline. Push straight down until each rod touches the cake board. Repeat procedure for every stacked cake used, except top cake.

5 Position next smallest cake on bottom cake, centering exactly. Position any other cakes in the same way. To stabilize cakes further, sharpen one end of a longer dowel rod and push it through all cakes and boards to the base of the bottom cake.

Working with Color

Combining several colors on your cake is part of the fun of fondant decorating. It's easy to tint white fondant just about any color you can imagine.

Tinting Fondant

Tint a small ball or enough to cover a whole cake—the important thing is to add just a little of the concentrated icing color at a time, until you arrive at the exact shade you want. If you'd rather not mix color yourself, you can purchase fondant in a variety of pre-tinted pastel, primary, neon, and natural shades.

1 Roll fondant into a ball, kneading until it's soft and pliable. Using a toothpick, add dots of icing color in several spots.

2 Knead color into your fondant ball; be sure to wear gloves to keep your hands stain-free.

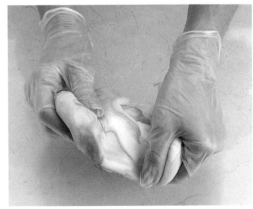

3 Continue kneading until color is evenly blended; add a little more color if needed.

Marbleizing

This subtle color treatment is an easy way to add richness to your cake. You can marbleize using white fondant with icing color or blend together white with pre-tinted fondant.

USING ICING COLOR

1 Roll fondant into a ball, kneading until it's soft and pliable. Using a toothpick, add dots of icing color in several spots.

2 Knead fondant slightly until color begins to blend in, creating marbleized streaks. Roll out fondant to desired shape.

USING PRE-TINTED AND WHITE FONDANT

1 Roll a log each of tinted and white fondant. Twist one log around the other several times.

2 Knead fondant slightly until color begins to blend in, creating marbleized streaks. Roll out fondant to desired shape.

Striping

Small strips of colored fondant can be rolled together to create a dazzling multi-colored fondant piece. It's a great way to make clothing, wrapped packages, and other decorations stand out!

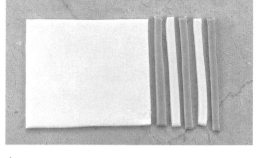

1 Roll out white fondant ⅛ inch thick and cut a base piece in desired size. Roll out various fondant colors ⅛ inch thick and cut strips in desired width.

2 Position strips on white base, so that edges meet. Using rolling pin, evenly roll out piece to ⅛ inch thick, so that edges and layers blend together.

3 Cut striped piece to desired size.

Cutting & Shaping Techniques

You're ready to give cakes a whole new dimension with fondant decorations you cut out or form by hand. To attach your fondant piece to your fondant cake, you either brush the back of the decoration lightly with water or with thinned fondant adhesive (p. 193).

Cut-Outs

Fondant has a texture like roll-out cookie dough so it's perfect for cutting as you would a cookie. Use gum paste cutters, available in a wide range of designs, or your favorite cookie cutters.

1 Roll out fondant ⅛ inches thick on mat lightly dusted with cornstarch.

2 Cut out desired shapes, pressing your cutter evenly through the fondant.

3 Remove any excess fondant around the edges. Lift shape with a spatula. Position shape as needed.

Overlays

Many gum paste cutters or cookie cutter sets come in graduated shapes, making it easy to top one fondant shape with a smaller one. It's a great way to create fantasy flowers with different color centers.

1 Separately roll out two different colors of fondant, ⅛ inches thick, on a mat lightly dusted with cornstarch.

2 Cut out desired shapes, using different size cutters. Remove any excess fondant around the edges. Lift shapes with a spatula.

3 Attach smaller shape to larger one with a damp brush.

Inlays

Using smaller cut outs or cookie cutters, it's easy to inlay a contrasting color shape within a larger cut shape. Inlays can also be done directly on your fondant-covered cake—just cut out a shape, then replace it with the same size shape in a different color.

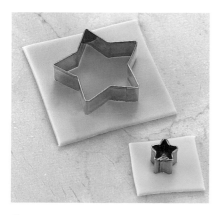

1 Separately roll out two different colors of fondant, ⅛ inches thick, on a mat lightly dusted with cornstarch. Cut out shapes using different size cutters.

2 Using the smaller cutter, cut a shape from the center of your larger cut shape. Lift out the piece with a toothpick.

3 Position the contrasting color piece inside the opening in your larger shape. For large inlays, lightly smooth area with a fondant smoother; for small inlays, smooth seams with your fingertip.

Curliques

You know how much flair curling ribbon adds to a package. Here's the easy way to make fondant curls.

1 Roll out fondant ¹/₁₆ inches thick on a mat lightly dusted with cornstarch. Cut into thin strips.

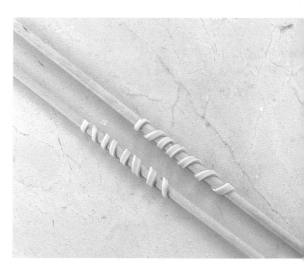

2 Loosely wrap strips several times around a dowel rod to form curls. Let set 5 to 10 minutes.

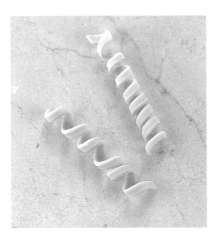

3 Slide curl off dowel rod and let dry. Attach to cake with damp brush.

Bows

Nothing says "celebrate" like a cake topped with a lush fondant bow. While the bow looks intricate, it's really just a grouping of fondant strips, folded, wrapped and arranged to create a full effect.

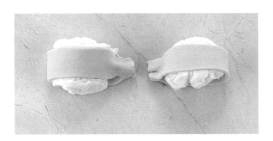

1 Cut strips for bow loops and streamers, using dimensions listed in project instructions. Your bow may use more loops than shown here or it may omit the bow center. Cut ends of stream-ers in a v-shape; set streamers aside on waxed paper dusted with cornstarch. Fold strips over to form loops. Brush ends lightly with damp brush. Align ends and pinch slightly to secure. Stuff loops with crushed facial tissue. Let dry.

2 Cut strip for bow center, if needed, following dimensions in project instructions. Wrap strip around the ends of two loops to create a knot look, attaching with damp brush.

3 Attach streamers under loops with damp brush.

Draping

You can't do this with any other icing! The luxurious folds of a fon-dant drape add richness as a side garland or as skirt accents. Be sure not to roll fondant too thin—the weight of the drape may tear the ends.

1 Roll out fondant ⅛ inches thick on a mat lightly dusted with cornstarch. Cut rectangles in sizes and number stated in cake instructions.

2 Immediately gather the short ends and pinch together to form drapes. Trim ends with scissors to taper if needed.

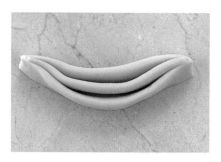

3 Attach drapes to cake by brushing back with water.

Ruffles

A ruffle can be gently flowing or tightly gathered as shown here. To create a softer looking ruffle, after cutting your fondant section, roll the ball tool, dipped in cornstarch, along one edge.

1 Roll out fondant ⅛ inches thick on a mat lightly dusted with cornstarch. Cut a strip following size stated in cake instructions. As a general rule, you will need a strip two to three times the length of the size of the finished ruffle.

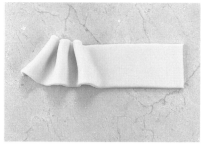

2 Starting on left side, fold small sections of the strip together vertically to form individual ruffles. As a section is done, continue adding strips by tucking cut end under the previous ruffle. Continue forming ruffles as needed.

3 Attach ruffle to cake by brushing top with water.

Leaves

Natural looking leaves can make your fondant bouquet come alive. Use a veining tool to mark vein lines, and let leaves dry on flower formers to form a lifelike curved shape.

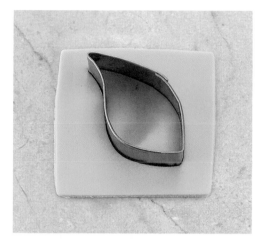

1 Roll out fondant ⅛ inches thick on a mat lightly dusted with cornstarch. Cut leaves using cookie cutters or cutters from a gum paste decorating set.

2 Place leaf on thin foam. Using a veining tool, mark vein lines, starting with center line. Add branch veins on both sides of center vein.

3 Remove leaf from foam and let dry. For curved leaves, dry on flower formers dusted with cornstarch.

Cupped Flowers

These little blossoms can go anywhere—on vines, as a side garland or on wires as part of a cake top bouquet. Make them ahead of time and let them dry in a pretty cupped shape.

1 Roll out fondant ⅛ inches thick on a mat lightly dusted with cornstarch. Cut flowers using cookie cutters or gum paste cutters. Transfer flowers one at a time to thin foam. Use a ball tool to soften edges by gently moving tool on edge of petal.

2 Transfer each flower to thick foam. Use a ball tool or dog bone tool to form a cupped shape by depressing tool in center of flower.

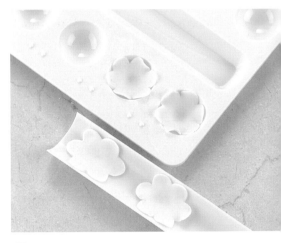

3 Let flowers dry in flower formers dusted with cornstarch or in candy melting plate sections. Add a dot to center using buttercream or royal icing or add a small ball of fondant for center.

Ribbon Roses

These quick-and-easy flowers can be placed on your cake right after you roll them. It's amazing how a few turns of your fondant strip can result in the realistic folds of a rose. Add fondant or buttercream leaves to create a full bouquet.

1 Roll out fondant ⅛ inch thick on a mat lightly dusted with cornstarch. Cut a 1 x 5 in. strip.

2 Begin rolling lightly from one end, gradually loosening roll as flower gets larger. Fold cut edge under.

3 Trim flower to desired height with scissors.

Full Bloom Roses

This may be your proudest moment with fondant! When you can hand-shape a rose this realistic using simple cut-out shapes, you'll know fondant is the easiest icing for decorating a cake. Make sure to add 1 teaspoon gum tragicanth for each 12 oz. fondant so the petals stand up and curl properly.

1 In advance: Make the rose center. Roll a ½-inch ball of fondant and form into a teardrop shape. Coat the end of a toothpick with vegetable shortening, insert into bottom of rose center; let dry at least 24 hours.

2 Roll fondant ¹⁄₁₆ inch thick on a mat lightly dusted with cornstarch. Using a large rose cutter, cut three blossom shapes. Cover two of the blossoms with plastic wrap and set aside. On remaining blossom, use a spatula to make a ½ inch cut between each petal toward middle of blossom. Place on thin foam and use a ball tool to soften edges of petals. Move blossom to thick foam and form a cup shape by pressing lightly in middle with ball tool.

3 Brush the middle of blossom with water. Insert the toothpick holding the rose center into the middle of the blossom and thread blossom up to the bottom of the rose center. Visualize the 5-petal blossom as a stick figure, with petals corresponding to "head," "arms" and "legs." Brush the "head" petal with water and wrap around rose center.

4 Brush one "arm" and opposite "leg" with water and fold up to cover the center bud. Repeat for remaining petals. Gently press bottom to shape. Pinch off any excess fondant from bottom. Furl back petal edges of the outer layer of petals.

5 Prepare the next blossom by making ½ inch cuts between each petal. Transfer to thin foam and use ball tool to soften petal edges. Transfer to thick foam and use ball tool to cup the two "arm" petals. Turn over blossom and cup two "leg" petals and "head" petal. Turn over blossom again and cup the center. Brush with water and thread onto toothpick. Brush the two "arm" petals with water and attach, centering over the seams of the previous two petals.

6 Brush remaining petals with water and attach, spacing evenly. Press bottom to shape; pinch off excess if needed.

7 Prepare the last blossom by making ½ inch cuts between each petal. Transfer to thin foam. Use ball tool to soften petal edges. Transfer to thick foam. Using the ball tool, cup all petals. Turn blossom shape over and cup center. Brush center with water. Thread toothpick through the center of the blossom shape. Brush water inside petals as needed.

8 Turn rose over and let petals fall naturally into place. Gently press petals against the base to attach.

9 Roll out fondant 1/16 inch thick and cut calyx using a calyx cutter. Brush base of calyx with water and thread toothpick through center of calyx. Press to attach and let dry. Remove from toothpick.

Recipes

Rolled Fondant

When making fondant from scratch, be sure to prepare and tint enough fondant to cover and decorate your cake. As with any icing, tint colors at one time; matching colors later may be difficult.

To save time and effort, you can purchase boxes of ready-made rolled fondant available in white, or conveniently pre-mixed in pastel, primary, neon, and natural colors.

2 envelopes or 1 tablespoon and 2 teaspoons unflavored gelatin

¼ cup cold water

½ cup glucose

2 tablespoons solid vegetable shortening

1 tablespoon glycerin

Icing color and flavoring, as desired

8 cups sifted confectioner's sugar (about 2 lbs.)

Combine gelatin and cold water; let stand until gelatin is softened. Place gelatin mixture in top of double boiler and heat until dissolved. Add glucose; mix well. Stir in shortening and just before completely melted, remove from heat. Add glycerin, flavoring and color. Cool until lukewarm. Next, place 4 cups (1 pound) confectioner's sugar in a bowl and make a well. Pour the lukewarm gelatin mixture into the well and stir with a wooden spoon, mixing in sugar and adding more, a little at a time, until stickiness disappears. Knead in remaining sugar. Knead until the fondant is smooth, pliable, and does not stick to your hands. If fondant is too soft, add more sugar; if too stiff, add water (a drop at a time). Use fondant immediately or store in airtight container in a cool dry place. Do not refrigerate or freeze. When ready to use, knead again until soft. This recipe yields approximately 36 oz., enough to cover a 10 x 4 inch high round cake.

Thinned Fondant Adhesive

Use this mixture when attaching dried fondant to other fondant decorations or for attaching freshly-cut fondant pieces to lollipop sticks or florist wire.

1 oz. ready-to-use rolled fondant (1½ inch ball)

¼ teaspoon water

Knead water into fondant until it becomes softened and sticky. To attach a fondant decoration, place mixture in decorating bag fitted with a small round tip, or brush on back of decoration. Recipe may be doubled.

Buttercream Icing

½ cup solid vegetable shortening

½ cup butter or margarine*

1 teaspoon clear vanilla extract

4 cups sifted confectioner's sugar (approx. 1 lb.)

2 tablespoons milk**

Cream butter and shortening with electric mixer. Add vanilla. Gradually add sugar, one cup at a time, beating well on medium speed. Scrape sides and bottom of bowl often. When all sugar has been mixed in, icing will appear dry. Add milk and beat at medium speed until light and fluffy. Keep bowl covered with a damp cloth until ready to use. For best results, keep icing bowl in refrigerator when not in use. Refrigerated in an airtight container, this icing can be stored 2 weeks. Rewhip before using. Makes 3 cups.

*Substitute all-vegetable shortening and ½ teaspoon butter flavoring to create pure white icing with a stiffer consistency.

**Add 3-4 tablespoons light corn syrup per recipe to thin for icing cake smooth.

Templates

Unity Candle (taper), page 26

Unity Candle (pillar), page 25
Cascading Pearl Favor Box, page 22

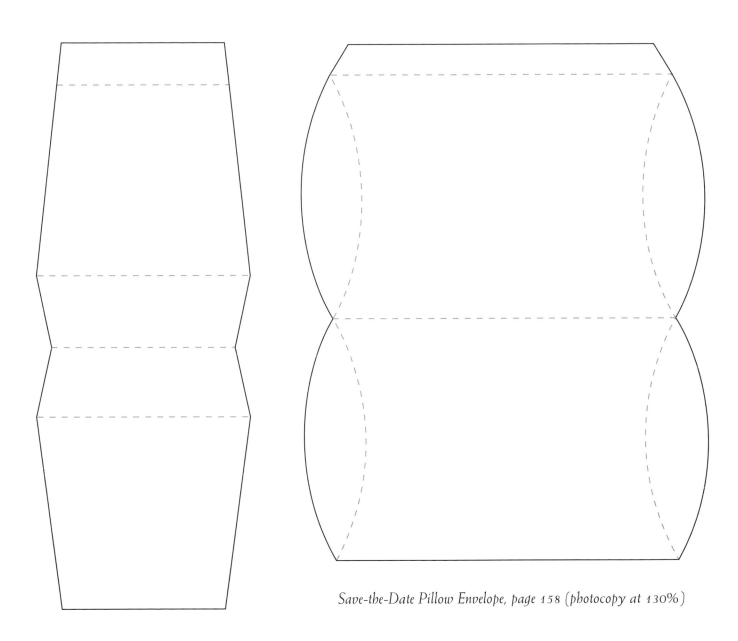

Save-the-Date Pillow Envelope, page 158 (photocopy at 130%)

Thank You Card, page 164 (photocopy at 130%)

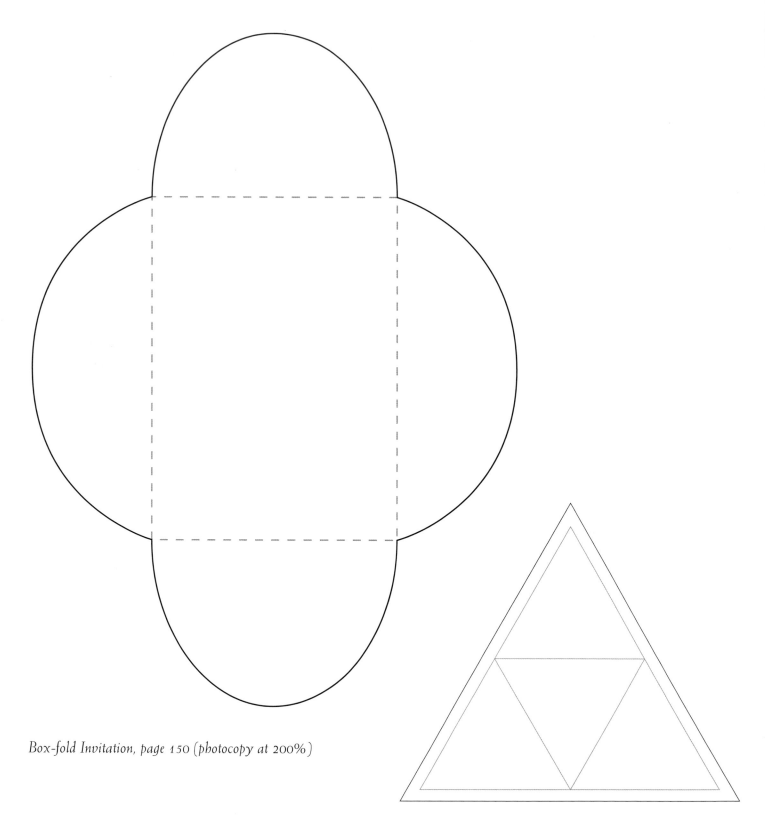

Box-fold Invitation, page 150 (photocopy at 200%)

Pyramidal Candy Box, page 156 (photocopy at 200%)

Metric Conversion Table

Inches	Decimal Inches	Rounded Metric	Inches	Decimal Inches	Rounded Metric	Inches	Decimal Inches	Rounded Metric
1/16	.0625	1.6 mm/.16 cm	7-1/2	7.5	19 cm	18		45.7 cm
1/8	.0125	3 mm/.3 cm	7-3/4	7.75	19.7 cm	18-1/4	18.25	46.4 cm
3/16	.1875	5 mm/.5 cm	8		20.3 cm	18-1/2	18.5	47 cm
1/4	.25	6 mm/.6 cm	8-1/4	8.25	21 cm	18-3/4	18.75	47.6 cm
5/16	.3125	8 mm/.8 cm	8-1/2	8.5	21.6 cm	19		48.3 cm
3/8	.375	9.5 mm/.95 cm	8-3/4	8.75	22.2 cm	19-1/4	19.25	48.9 cm
7/16	.4375	1.1 cm	9		22.9 cm	19-1/2	19.5	49.5 cm
1/2	.5	1.3 cm	9-1/4	9.25	23.5 cm	19-3/4	19.75	50.2 cm
9/16	.5625	1.4 cm	9-1/2	9.5	24.1 cm	20		50.8 cm
5/8	.625	1.6 cm	9-3/4	9.75	24.8 cm	20-1/4	20.25	51.4 cm
11/16	.6875	1.7 cm	10		25.4 cm	20-1/2	20.5	52.1 cm
3/4	.75	1.9 cm	10-1/4	10.25	26 cm	20-3/4	20.75	52.7 cm
13/16	.8125	2.1 cm	10-1/2	10.5	26.7 cm	21		53.3 cm
7/8	.875	2.2 cm	10-3/4	10.75	27.3 cm	21-1/4	21.25	54 cm
15/16	.9375	2.4 cm	11		27.9 cm	21-1/2	21.5	54.6 cm
			11-1/4	11.25	28.6 cm	21-3/4	21.75	55.2 cm
1		2.5 cm	11-1/2	11.5	29.2 cm	22		55.9 cm
1-1/4	1.25	3.2 cm	11-3/4	11.75	30 cm	22-1/4	22.25	56.5 cm
1-1/2	1.5	3.8 cm	12		30.5 cm	22-1/2	22.5	57.2 cm
1-3/4	1.75	4.4 cm	12-1/4	12.25	31.1 cm	22-3/4	22.75	57.8 cm
2		5 cm	12-1/2	12.5	31.8 cm	23		58.4 cm
2-1/4	2.25	5.7 cm	12-3/4	12.75	32.4 cm	23-1/4	23.25	59 cm
2-1/2	2.5	6.4 cm	13		33 cm	23-1/2	23.5	59.7 cm
2-3/4	2.75	7 cm	13-1/4	13.25	33.7 cm	23-3/4	23.75	60.3 cm
3		7.6 cm	13-1/2	13.5	34.3 cm	24		61 cm
3-1/4	3.25	8.3 cm	13-3/4	13.75	35 cm	24-1/4	24.25	61.6 cm
3-1/2	3.5	8.9 cm	14		35.6 cm	24-1/2	24.5	62.2 cm
3-3/4	3.75	9.5 cm	14-1/4	14.25	36.2 cm	24-3/4	24.75	62.9 cm
4		10.2 cm	14-1/2	14.5	36.8 cm	25		63.5 cm
4-1/4	4.25	10.8 cm	14-3/4	14.75	37.5 cm	25-1/4	25.25	64.1 cm
4-1/2	4.5	11.4 cm	15		38.1 cm	25-1/2	25.5	64.8 cm
4-3/4	4.75	12 cm	15-1/4	15.25	38.7 cm	25-3/4	25.75	65.4 cm
5		12.7 cm	15-1/2	15.5	39.4 cm	26		66 cm
5-1/4	5.25	13.3 cm	15-3/4	15.75	40 cm	26-1/4	26.25	66.7 cm
5-1/2	5.5	14 cm	16		40.6 cm	26-1/2	26.5	67.3 cm
5-3/4	5.75	14.6 cm	16-1/4	16.25	41.3 cm	26-3/4	26.75	68 cm
6		15.2 cm	16-1/2	16.5	41.9 cm	27		68.6 cm
6-1/4	6.25	15.9 cm	16-3/4	16.75	42.5 cm	27-1/4	27.25	69.2 cm
6-1/2	6.5	16.5 cm	17		43.2 cm	27-1/2	27.5	69.9 cm
6-3/4	6.75	17.1 cm	17-1/4	17.25	43.8 cm	27-3/4	27.75	70.5 cm
7		17.8 cm	17-1/2	17.5	44.5 cm	28		71.1 cm
7-1/4	7.25	18.4 cm	17-3/4	17.75	45.1 cm			

Project Designers

Brandy Logan

Brandy Logan is a fanatical scrapbooker living in the mountains of NC with her husband Clayton and their two sons, Hayden and Emerson. She stumbled into the hobby of scrapbooking while attending college at NC State University back in 1999 and has never looked back. Brandy's work has appeared in many publications and she has worked with several online design teams. You can see her work at www.twopeasinabucket.com/userprofile.asp?user_id=7401 or contact her by email at thelogans@mchsi.com.

Joan K. Morris

Joan K. Morris's artistic endeavors have led her down many successful creative paths, including costume design for motion pictures, and ceramics. Joan has contributed projects for numerous Lark books, including, *Beautiful Ribbon Crafts, Gifts For Baby, Halloween: A Grown-ups Guide to Creative Costumes, Creating Fantastic Vases, Hardware Style, Michaels Book of Crafts, Hip Handbags,* and many more.

Terry Taylor

Terry Taylor lends his creative spirit full time to Lark Books. In his spare time, he glues, pastes, and otherwise assembles works of art using a wide range of media from old cds to broken china. His current interests include metal jewelry. His work has been exhibited in many galleries and in many publications.

Linda Kopp

Linda Kopp is a general jack-of-all-crafts dabbling in pottery, stained glass, mosaics, painting, and school dioramas. When not harassing her two young sons to finish their homework, she enjoys getting her hands dirty—either through crafting or gardening. She lives, thrives, and hikes in the soul-soothing mountains outside of Asheville, NC.

Pamela Frye Hauer

Pamela Frye Hauer earned a degree in Visual Communications and worked in the fields of photography, graphic design, and special event planning before becoming professionally involved in the scrapbooking industry in 1999. Since then, she has created ideas, artwork, and projects for numerous publications and companies, including *Memory Makers Magazine.* She co-authored the scrapbooking book, *Montage Memories* and her own memory craft book, *Memories in Miniature,* was recently released. She lives in Colorado with her husband and two young sons.

Trudy Sigurdson

Trudy Sigurdson had been an avid rubber stamper for about two years when she walked into a scrapbook store for the first time and her obsession instantly changed from stamping to scrapbooking. Now she has been scrapbooking for more than four years and has successfully turned a hobby into a full time career as an independent designer and instructor. Trudy's work has been featured in numerous scrapbooking and craft publications, and she is currently working on her first solo authored book, which will be released in spring '06. When she's not traveling throughout North America teaching at various trade shows and conventions, Trudy can be found teaching at her local scrapbook store in Victoria B.C., Canada where she lives with her two children, Aysha and Alex .

Juanita Mantel

Juanita is a self-taught cake decorator who has been baking and designing cakes for over 40 years. She is one of approximately 30 cake decorators nationwide to be certified by the Retail Bakers Association. Juanita owns The Bake Shoppe (www.bakeshoppeasheville.com) in Asheville, N.C., which specializes in custom-decorated wedding and birthday cakes. In addition to award-winning cakes, Juanita and daughter Heidi Bryson also bake and decorate a wide variety of cookies and pies.

Index

Acknowledgments

Many thanks and much appreciation to the persons who helped make this book happen: Wilton Industries, Inc., (wilton.com), for graciously sharing their photography and invaluable cake decorating expertise featured in the "Working with Fondant" section, in addition to the use of their 12 month wedding planner; Carol Taylor and Deborah Morgenthal for their invaluable guidance; Megan Kirby and Dawn Cusick for showing me the ropes; Terry Taylor for his crafty ways; Keith Wright, a fellow Texan, for making miracles; Val Anderson whose thoroughness words cannot express; Cathy Franczyk and Daniel Masini for their professionalism, promptness, and overall pleasant demeanor; Kim Lewis for lending an ear (as always); Chris Kopp for his unerring computer skills and endless moral support; and lastly, I'm extremely grateful to the many contributing writers and designers for their quick pace and tireless efforts.

—Linda Kopp

Look for these other wedding-on-a-budget books from Lark Crafts:

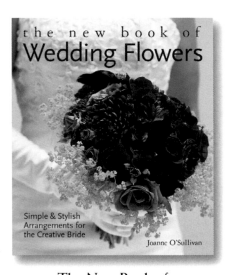

**Make It in Minutes
Wedding Crafts**
Catherine Risling
ISBN 9781600592287

**Pretty Weddings for
Practically Pennies**
Catherine Risling
ISBN 9781402713484

**The New Book of
Wedding Flowers**
Simple & Stylish Arrangements
for the Creative Bride
Joanne O'Sullivan
ISBN 9781579909604

LARK BOOKS

A Division of Sterling Publishing Co., Inc.
New York / London

It's all on www.larkbooks.com

Can't find the materials you need to create a project?
Search our database for craft suppliers & sources for hard-to-find materials.

Got an idea for a book?
Read our book proposal guidelines and contact us.

Want to show off your work?
Browse current calls for entries.

Want to know what new and exciting books we're working on?
Sign up for our free e-newsletter.

Feeling crafty?
Find free, downloadable project directions on the site.

Interested in learning more about the authors, designers & editors who create Lark books?